Advance Praise for *You've Been VALidated*

"I have known Val for many years. What never ceases to amaze me is that whenever I am in her company, she manages to introduce me to new people that she inevitably knows will be mutually beneficial. Her energy is contagious, and people simply want to be in her orbit, and that includes me!"

–Laura Gellar, Founder Laura Gellar Beauty

"Val is the QUEEN of lifting people up and connecting others. Her energy is quite literally infectious and what's truly special is she makes everyone around her a better version of themselves with her positivity. I'm so excited for her to share her secret sauce with the world in this book."

–Eva Pilgrim, ABC News

"Val is a truly warm, kind and giving human! To know Val is to love her, I'm proud to say I've been 'VALidated.'"

–Bevy Smith, Television Personality

YOU'VE BEEN VALIDATED

YOU'VE BEEN VALIDATED

A PLAYBOOK FOR CONFIDENCE AND CONNECTION

VALERIE GREENBERG

A POST HILL PRESS BOOK
ISBN: 979-8-89565-008-0
ISBN (eBook): 979-8-89565-009-7

You've Been VALidated:
A Playbook for Confidence and Connection

Cover design by Jim Villaflores

Post Hill Press
New York • Nashville
posthillpress.com

Published in the United States of America
1 2 3 4 5 6 7 8 9 10

TABLE OF CONTENTS

INTRODUCTION

#youvebeenVALidated, my lifestyle brand's purpose, is to inspire you to channel the most confident version of yourself and encourage everyone to step out of their comfort zone and create meaningful connections with others. My mission in writing this book is to enable you to cultivate your own path to validation. By sharing my journey of ups and downs as a media personality, and tapping into my personal network of heavy hitting celebrities, influencers and thought leaders, you will learn how to advocate for yourself and develop meaningful relationships. I have always embraced my strengths of being able to read a room and ability to approach and talk to anyone regardless of their social status. My network of friends and business associates reach out regularly knowing I can make a powerful introduction in a wide array of professional fields.

My natural ability to befriend new people, lift their spirits and affect them positively are skills that have served me in my many professional opportunities. In life, everyone encounters hard times that are out of their control. Candid narratives from my close network of friends, who I refer to as my ***"Confidence Community,"*** are included throughout the book. Challenges faced which led to growth and new opportunities will leave you inspired. Something you initially saw as a setback will only occur as a small glitch and push you further upward on your journey. You will learn how to navigate the environment around you and garner the respect you deserve in both your personal and professional life by discovering your VALU. #youvebeen-VALidated, pass it on!

CHAPTER ONE

MEET MY *"CONFIDENCE COMMUNITY"*

The members of my ***"Confidence Community"*** are listed below with a brief description of how we met and their achievements. Building an open circle of friends that you have admiration for is a key element in creating a forum for growth, both personally and professionally. Developing this type of community offers the space to bounce advice off one another and serves as an incredible support system. My ***"Confidence Community"*** is part of my inner circle that I have learned from and respect a great deal. I am thrilled to share the quotes, knowledge, and expertise they have provided throughout the material, as you embark on your journey to building genuine connections and achieving confidence. Everyone can benefit from inspiration and motivation, and I hope the included quotes will offer you that.

MEET ISAAC BOOTS

Celebrity fitness personality Isaac Boots played a pivotal role in my exercise routine throughout the pandemic. Isaac offered his challenging TORCH'D workout classes for free on Instagram. He had his celebrity friends like Vanessa Hudgens and Lisa Rinna participate in his livestreams. Having affected me so profoundly, we began messaging back and forth on Instagram. When by chance we were dining at the same restaurant, I took it upon myself to walk over to him and introduce myself. We embrace each other's energy and align with our outlook on encouraging others to be the best version of themselves.

MEET HARRY CARSON

National Football League legend Harry Carson, former captain of the New York Giants football team, and I originally met when I was just a toddler, accompanying my father to watch Harry practice at his team's summer training camp. My dad was a huge football fan who had a lot to say from the sidelines. Harry and I reconnected during my adult years at "The Hamptons Happening Fundraiser," supporting The Samuel Waxman Cancer Research Foundation. We now consider each other great friends and he is an integral part of my ***"Confidence Community."***

MEET VERNON DAVIS

Super Bowl champion turned actor Vernon Davis and I met in the green room at the Fox 5 television station in Washington, D.C. It was the day before Thanksgiving, and we were booked on the same panel to comment on the pop culture headlines of the day on *Good Day DC*. When he introduced himself, I remembered him as a contestant on *Dancing with the Stars*. I immediately took a liking to and had a lot of respect for Vernon as my mom and I sat and chatted with him. He is extremely accomplished in a variety of fields, since he is also an actor, author, and philanthropist, and I am elated he has agreed to be part of this book and is open to sharing his personal practices.

MEET TAYLOR DAYNE

Taylor Dayne is an eighties pop icon, Grammy nominee, and singer of such hit songs as "Tell It to My Heart." The two of us became friends (or, shall I say, more like family) early on in my career, when she was a client at the public relations firm where I was working. She has been the most supportive friend, always having my back in my personal and professional lives. Any venture I was a part of throughout developing my career, big or small, she was the first to cheer me on and participate as talent. She has spent time with me and my family while on vacation in Santa Barbara and is like a sister I can always count on.

MEET COUNTESS LUANN DE LESSEPS

Countess Luann de Lesseps came into many people's lives as an original *Real Housewife of New York*. She and I had several interactions running into each other at social engagements in New York City. Our friendship flourished after we sat down and had lunch together a few years before I started writing this book. I am in awe of her work ethic and have such admiration for the pride she takes in truly entertaining her fans. With so many different projects under her belt, from television to live touring, Countess Luann is conquering the entertainment world like a queen.

MEET PAULA FROELICH

Paula Froelich's name is synonymous with breaking entertainment news, having previously run *The New York Post*'s gossip column Page Six. She is a pioneer when it comes to celebrity journalism. When I noticed her at the Union Square Greenmarket in New York City, I approached her, and we've been friends ever since. She is someone who I respect and look up to and I am so happy she has joined me as a member of my ***"Confidence Community."***

MEET JULIA HAART

As a "girl on the glow," (a phrase I associate with spreading actionable positivity and cheer while out and about) I kept seeing Julia Haart at social events. I recognized her from her show on Netflix, *My Unorthodox Life*. Julia is an advocate, philanthropist, and trailblazer in the fashion community. Little did I know she would have a profound influence on me and become one of my closest friends and confidantes. I am honored that Julia is so graciously opening up to me as a member of my ***"Confidence Community."***

MEET TY HUNTER

Ty and I became friends after connecting in a shared Uber Pool, yet another opportunity I found to make a connection and a new friend. Ty is one of the most sought-after talents in the fashion industry, having emerged on the scene as Beyoncé's stylist. When I created a digital web series for a fashion magazine, he was kind enough to come on as a celebrity guest. Having him join my ***"Confidence Community"*** was a no-brainer.

MEET DR. ROBI LUDWIG

Dr. Robi Ludwig and I met when she was contributing to a magazine I had been featured in highlighting my lifestyle expertise. She is a psychotherapist, author, and familiar face that pops up on network television regularly discussing mental health. We had been at the same various gatherings in celebration of the publication and soon realized we had mutual friends. I already had an immense amount of respect for her, as she was conquering the mental health, television, and true crime space all at once. As our friendship grew organically, I was drawn to her warmhearted nature and constant support in building me up whenever tough life circumstances would arise. I am honored that she allowed me to interview her and is sharing her wealth of knowledge with my readers to shed light from a mental health perspective.

MEET DALE MOSS

Dale Moss (whose name you may recognize from *The Bachelorette* franchise) and I met at a mutual friend's barbeque. Dale has played in the NFL, models professionally, is an actor, documentarian, fitness influencer, ambassador for the Special Olympics, and my incredibly supportive friend. He is by definition a go-getter, and I am so happy to be able to include him in the book.

MEET DR. PIMPLE POPPER

My friend Dr. Sandra Lee, who most people recognize as Dr. Pimple Popper (from her viral TikTok shorts and series on TLC) and I met at a press dinner she was hosting showcasing her newest product line. Our bond was instant, as we took notice of our shared fun, silly, not taking ourselves too seriously, everyday outlooks. In fact, she bestowed the greatest compliment upon me when she told me I reminded her of her best friend.

MEET JEN SELTER

I met my beautiful, fit, fierce, Instagram influencer, and innovator friend Jen Selter face to face when our taxi cabs pulled up to The Alice + Olivia Pride Party at the exact same time. From the moment the cab doors opened, we realized what we had in common: the love for our mothers. You see, her mom and I met years prior, and her mom has always been so supportive, making the sweetest comments on my social media accounts. My friendship with Jen has since flourished and we continue to empower each other.

MEET ROB SHUTER

My dear friend Rob Shuter has provided guidance to me throughout my entire career. He brings so many achievements to the table as a former celebrity publicist, author, innovator, and creating his own celebrity platform Naughty Gossip. He is a television host, podcaster, and the go-to celebrity expert on entertainment news programs across the globe. Rob is an incredible storyteller, and has been a friend I've learned from, collaborated with, and provided me with a whole lot of laughter. He's always been supportive, and I am so excited he agreed to offer his insight for this book and as a member of my ***"Confidence Community."***

MEET BEVY SMITH

Bevy Smith and I were at an influencer dinner when we first met. A couple of years later, I was cast as a lifestyle expert on *Page Six TV*, and Bevy was one of the cohosts. We had the opportunity to work together, and being on set together was always such a blast. She is a successful television and radio host, best-selling author, public speaker, and a ray of sunshine. I'm so lucky she is a part of my ***"Confidence Community."***

MEET ADAM WEITSMAN

Initially, I became aware of entrepreneur, investor, and recycler Adam Weitsman when my colleague at the television show *Inside Edition* pointed out his philanthropic and charitable endeavors. Our friendship grew via FaceTime and through social media, reaching new heights during the pandemic, when he graciously agreed to join me as the celebrity guest on my Instagram live series. Finally, the universe brought us together in person when I literally bumped into him at Global Citizen Festival. As in demand as Adam is, he always makes himself available to me for advice and is someone I know I can count on. Needless to say, I am over the moon that he took time out of his busy schedule and agreed to allow me to share his insight with my readers as part of this book.

MEET BEVY SMITH

Bevy Smith and I were at an influencer dinner when we first met a couple of years later. [illegible] a lifestyle [illegible] Sirius XM, and Bevy was one of the [illegible]. We had the opportunity to work together, and being [illegible] together was always such a blast. She's a [illegible] television and radio host, a bestselling author, public speaker, and a [illegible] her own show "Confidence Company."

MEET [illegible]

[illegible]

CHAPTER TWO

BE YOUR OWN BEST FRIEND

"Be Your Own Best Friend" is a phrase that my mother instilled in me as early as I can remember, and one that remains just as powerful today. Oftentimes, we subconsciously insert roadblocks on our path, which clearly makes our trip more difficult. We have to remind ourselves that we are in the driver's seat when it comes to achievements in both our personal and professional lives. Why create more traffic and noise that keeps us at a standstill or in a holding pattern? We all dislike being stuck on the highway, so don't place yourself in that position when it comes to living your everyday life.

At times, I have been afraid to face emotions and feelings that make me uncomfortable. In those situations, the fear of the feelings can be more troublesome than the actual feelings themselves. When we allow our day-to-day stress to overwhelm us instead of being focused on the present, we are doing ourselves a disservice and being counterproductive. If we accept the challenges we are met with, really embrace them and allow them to soak deeply into every layer of our being, we will persevere. Learning to respond instead of react when circumstances are tough is a challenge we can meet together. It's not an easy one, but it can be done with willpower and a positive attitude. This is something everyone who needs a little encouragement can benefit from.

I utilize many strategies in an effort to go easier on myself, which I find synonymous with self-care: I practice yoga, meditate, jog several times a week, and treat myself to an occasional massage. I also follow a healthy diet plan, which elevates my self-worth, while still allowing myself a cheat day every once in a while. It truly is all about balance.

I even started taking more baths, finding the warm soak extremely soothing, and I found and joined a community of people that relish recovery time and cold plunges as much as I do, as well as turning to self-help literature in an effort to constantly better myself. Some choose to listen to podcasts and/or watch reality television to unwind and decompress.

The bottom line is there are no wrong strategies; just implement what works best for you. It may take time, but all of these actions to be kind to yourself are essential to your well-being.

Stop beating yourself up when you need to take a break. Living in New York City and being as social as I am has linked me with a lot of influential people that I highly respect and look to regularly for advice and encouragement. Taking a moment and pressing pause is a common recommendation I've received from many celebrities, influencers, and successful business people I have become close with when I've asked them how they find time for themselves in their busy lives. Giving yourself a time-out when you need one and slowing down so you don't get overwhelmed could be just what you need to push that reset button and see things from a clear and positive perspective.

Feeling good about yourself is necessary for reflecting and receiving positive energy. Getting yourself to a point of burnout is not going to be good for you or anyone that you care for. Being your own best friend isn't something where you snap your fingers and it happens instantly: it takes effort and commitment. Whenever I step onto the yoga mat, my instructor says, "Let go of what is no longer serving you." Incorporating the yogi philosophy takes discipline and the repetition is extraordinarily helpful when it comes to eliminating overthinking and ruminating on obsessive thoughts. It allows me to feel lighter emotionally. Everyone has their own set of underlying "stuff" and these are some ways you can lighten your load to begin a lifelong journey of a best friendship with yourself.

What is your professional opinion on the importance of being kind to yourself and practicing self-care?

Dr. Robi Ludwig: "As a psychotherapist, I understand the value of engaging in self-care and being kind to oneself. The issue with these terms is that it can be challenging for individuals to interpret what this actually means for themselves. The concept of self-care and being kind to oneself can vary greatly from person to person. When I think about being good to oneself, from an analyst's perspective, I conceptualize it as making healthy and positive choices for oneself. The quality of our lives is largely based on the decisions we make. Learning how to create a life that is healthy and fulfilling involves considering the opportunities and/or consequences of the choices we make."

Val's thoughts: "Dr. Robi's answer truly resonates with me as I try to navigate my day-to-day by making good choices. If I do slip up, however, I try not to be too hard on myself about it."

Remember: it's a marathon, not a sprint is a phrase that strongly resonates with me. Do I consider myself successful? Absolutely! Was this always the case? No! Meeting my dreams and goals has always been a priority, and even though I have felt frustrated along the journey, I was determined to turn what I was passionate about into my profession. I have now come to realize that my effort and giving it my all is truly what constitutes success.

The old adage about hard work paying off rings true. You have to be patient, learn your craft, and become an expert. In my case, I had to pick up work outside of my career field in an effort to pay my bills. I used this as an opportunity to build on my communication skills instead of letting it throw me off course as I continued in pursuit of my goals. There are in fact still plenty of difficult days and sacrifices to be made. The journey continues on and I look forward to what comes next!

It took me quite some time to get to a playing field I felt I was deserving of, but I am proof it is possible and now I want to help others who have that fire burning inside of them turn their passion into a career as well.

There is no one universal formula that people can turn to in order to learn how to pursue their passion; however, you can develop your own unique individual approach. This can be curated for every individual with the guidance, expertise, and tools this book will equip you with. Recognizing that results don't take place overnight is an essential part of the process.

What do you say to individuals that are in a hurry or impatient when it comes to meeting their professional goals?

Adam Weitsman: "The long race seems to be something that lasts forever; it is very difficult to make quick success in this day and age even though there are some exceptions."

Val's thoughts: "Not seeing immediate results is challenging for me at times. Hearing someone as accomplished as Adam talk about the long game motivates me to keep going."

...

Dr. Pimple Popper: "You never know where life will take you; I've learned this from my patients as well. Life is long and the road is not often straight, so be patient and almost all the time, what will be, will be."

Val's thoughts: "Dr. Pimple Popper's reminder helps me to be more at ease with uncertainty."

Acting on my curiosity opens many doors for me professionally. While working as a summer intern at Wenner Media, at the time the publishing home to magazines *Us Weekly* and *Rolling Stone*, I decided to work up the courage and walk through the office's open floor plan inquiring if anyone needed additional assistance. The worst result would be that I wouldn't have any traction on new opportunities, but to my surprise, the assistant editor was open to sending me out on assignments to interview celebrities. To get that opportunity, all I had to do was believe in myself, show interest, and ask. The following week I was at Capitale, an elegant New York City event space, interviewing the King of R&B, Usher, for my very first *Us Weekly* assignment. This benchmarked my first professional achievement.

Prior to graduating from the University of Florida with a degree in journalism, I spent countless hours researching and cold calling public relations firms in New York City. My hard work was rewarded when I reached someone who was willing to help. She was the assistant to the head of the New York office, and gave me a meeting, despite her busy schedule. At the time, there was no position available, but guess who found out when an opportunity did become available at that company? Me!

I ended up working at the firm for several years and learned invaluable insights that have remained instrumental in promoting myself and my projects to this day. The special bonds I formed with my colleagues there have transformed into lifelong friendships and chosen family, which then improved the quality of my everyday life. I still work with those friends, just in a different capacity, as I create content for their brands, highlight their clients on television, and consult for them in a broadcast scope. Opening myself up to these opportunities by seeking out new relationships, even at the novice stage of my career, proved to be a great way of being good to myself and being my own best friend!

While working as an executive assistant at the public relations firm, I found myself on a team project that was handling press for a film premiering at the Tribeca Film Festival. This was a very busy time for entertainment programs, so not every show had the ability to send coverage to certain press opportunities. I went for it and volunteered to interview our cast at the press junket. We then serviced the interviews to the entertainment shows that were not able to attend to secure more visibility for our client and project. This experience showed me how exciting being on camera was and pushed me toward pursuing my on camera presence.

After I left the public relations firm to pursue on-camera hosting, I came across a website with no presence of celebrity content being run out of a Midwestern city looking to enhance their entertainment value and score big name interviews. Aligning myself with this platform was strategic on my part since I needed a media outlet to partner with that was up and running and already disseminating content. In return, we received access to some of the most glamorous and exclusive New York Fashion Week events and interviews, churning out content based on my previous public relations connections and relationships. Getting creative was key, since the platform was partially smoke and mirrors.

My relationships, ability to connect with the talent, their representatives, and what I was producing content wise, were what was truly valuable. This allowed me to build my reel, a compilation of my best on camera work showcasing me as the host and interviewer. My access rested heavily on how I emanated confidence, since I knew it was the only way I could secure the access which led to the content.

Our paths could blow in any direction. Confidence and connection are essential to get you to the right location! Getting creative and not letting anyone pigeonhole you can be challenging, but if you want to work in an industry that can be cutthroat and difficult as ever to break into, you can't let anyone put you in a box or make you feel like you aren't deserving of the opportunities you get. It's important to remember that even when you aren't selected for the project, it just means it wasn't right for you.

I realized I was going to have to carve a path for myself. I knew what I wanted and was deserving of, and I would have to have my own back if I wanted to become on-air talent on a full-time basis. Handling myself by emitting confidence and asking questions with conviction enabled me to make the transition to hosting, despite having one of the least coveted spots on the red carpet and without the anchor or credibility of a well-known press outlet backing me. This was only temporary, and by paying my dues, my status shifted.

You never know who may be instrumental in helping you on your journey. I can cite many examples of times I approached and met people who became very pivotal in my life. For instance, I was commuting to work on the train one day, when I spotted a familiar face from my office and decided to introduce myself to her. She was the fashion editor for the magazine *Life & Style Weekly* where I was working but in a different department. As our business relationship evolved, we would brainstorm possible ways for me to transition to branding myself as a lifestyle expert. She graciously connected me with her friend's brand consulting firm that specialized in booking regional television segments in a variety of markets. I agreed to promote the brand consulting firm's clients on the segments and in exchange they would book me as a trade, which led to my gaining more credibility as on-air talent. Consistency and securing air time is essential if you are going to develop your presence and persona in the television and on camera space. It is of utmost importance to acknowledge those that are supportive and selflessly take time to help you. In my case, this friend played a pivotal role instilling confidence in me and in my career development. Her belief in me and making a connection and wanting nothing else but to see her friend succeed mattered.

All my unique and varied experiences and projects have helped to build out my résumé and furthered my appreciation for determination and hard work. The reality is these weren't always glamorous assignments: using vacation days from my administrative day job to be available to travel on a bus to Pennsylvania for a television segment was stressful. It took a lot of juggling to manage this multi-tasking gracefully. When I got there, my taxi cab began to roll backwards upon arrival at the television station, as it was located on a huge hill and I thought we were going to tumble right back into the woods. My motel accommodations when on the road presenting local segments were far from elegant. My goal was always to do this full time by booking bigger markets followed by national appearances and earning more money.

By sharing these anecdotes with you, I hope to provide inspiration to pound the pavement and not be discouraged during setbacks or challenges. Regardless of how many "no's" you may hear or emails that go unanswered, your focus should shift to the positive responses that flood your inbox and the future fantastic opportunities that will come your way. I got there and you can, too! This is all in the deck of playing cards when it comes to being your own best friend.

Breaking bad habits is crucial. They hold us back and once they are eliminated, you will have proved to yourself that you are capable of moving forward and making positive changes in your life. Every accomplishment helps to build confidence. It's important to accept that these vices will not go away overnight. It takes work just like anything else that is worth it in life. Think about what is triggering you to engage in this habit, then bring your attention to what you stand to gain by putting a halt on this habit. For example, let's say you are a stress eater. Think about how your digestion will improve and how you will feel better overall by eating slower and being more present when sitting down for a meal. Visualize the good that will come as a result of the willpower you harness. Come to terms that putting in the effort to change can make a difference and get you closer to your goal of kicking this bad habit to the curb.

Something that I have found very helpful with breaking bad habits is taking action and engaging in activities that can be attributed to bringing about happiness. Be sure to spend your time on the moments in your routine that you normally tend to rush through and actually take a moment to enjoy them. Our senses help ground us, so if the smell of your coffee is enjoyable, then take the time to really be in the moment when you brew it. Do not rush through tasks that may seem trivial; instead, be present and this will affect your whole mood for the better. Moving fast and checking off a to-do list is not the only way to be productive, and it has taken me a long time to realize this.

Being a person that moves quickly, I have to make a conscious effort to slow my pace down. Our mindset, rest, and recovery can get us to heights we never thought could be possible.

What is a bad habit you broke?

Adam Weitsman: "Being unorganized and having bad time management. I broke it by being very structured and getting rid of time-wasting activities."

Val's thought: "This type of discipline is something I have to work on daily."

...

Julia Haart: "I wasn't diligent and careful about contracts. I just assumed if people were your friends or your loved ones, that they would be trustworthy and honest. Do not make that assumption! Get the right contract, check, double-check and triple-check and be sure to use a good lawyer. Protect yourself and learn from my mistakes."

Val's thoughts: "I'm in complete agreement with Julia on this. Regardless of a friendship or work relationship, you need to have a legal professional make sure your agreement and contracts are in place and have your interests documented. It's the best way to protect yourself in business dealings."

Pick your battles and understand the importance of how you deliver your message. Everyone experiences stress in their lives. How you handle this stress determines how it affects your life decisions and well-being. When you start to obsess and overthink situations, that is when you can get yourself into trouble. Yes, it is important to acknowledge what is bothering you; however, be sure to look at the big picture before you react. When you are delivering your message, try to remain calm, despite the fact that the person you are interacting with may be causing you emotional turmoil. If in fact you come to the realization that whatever is irking you needs to be addressed, be sure to have all your ducks in a row so you can calmly paint a clear picture and the conversation doesn't get turned around on you. The last thing you want is the individual you are addressing to feel attacked and be defensive. When that happens, the message gets lost. When you have healthy relationships around you, your emotional health is better, which all circles back to being your own best friend.

Develop an inner circle that understands you. We are all unique and aligning our core values and interests can bring people together. Getting real with what you are going through can often be a gift for you and those around you. Revealing is a very powerful tool: it helps those important to you realize they are not alone when it comes to conquering personal hurdles.

Get good with being alone. Your relationship with yourself is the most important one you will have. Self-reflection gives you the space you need to grow. This comes more naturally to some and is more challenging for others. In fact, sometimes it is hard for me to sit down and focus because the fear of missing out is constantly lurking in the shadows. As an extrovert, I also happen to enjoy being around others, but I have come to realize my relationship with myself is the most important one. So, I suggest taking some alone time for yourself every day.

Being your own best friend also involves understanding that going through challenges is totally normal. Overachievers continually put pressure on themselves to have all of the answers and are guilty of feeling like they haven't accomplished enough when they don't know everything. It can be a vicious cycle, but remind yourself that if you are making a conscious effort and moving forward one day at a time in life, that is a win!

Don't be afraid to walk up to the most powerful player in the room and make the most of the opportunity. If you have access, be smart and utilize it. I have done this my entire life and it is usually received well. I have noticed how those around me are inspired to do the same when they witness it firsthand. When I approached the head of talent of a major network at a television premiere, he was completely open and responsive to my approach. Being in the present moment allowed me to recognize I had an opportunity. You don't want to miss out on who and what is right in front of you. These new relationships have led to my progress and advancements, and I am so happy I checked my fear at the door.

Getting overlooked happens. It is unfortunate and will likely occur many times throughout life. That is why a glass half full focus is so important. Early in my career, I experienced a particular situation that caused me to be upset and bitter for a long time. It took place at the same time I had made the decision to pursue my on-air television career. Having been struggling financially, my disappointment and the outcome of this situation was even harder for me to swallow.

I had connected a female fashion designer with a casting agent and she was subsequently selected as a cast member in a successful reality television show directly because of my introduction. I felt pushed to the wayside when my role in this connection was ignored. The negative emotion consumed me, and I allowed it to for far too long. This was counterproductive on my part and certainly not a way of being my own best friend.

Don't let your frustration fester. You have the power to transform it into a positive situation. In this case, a few years later, when coming face-to-face with her, she was kind, apologetic, and said I was single-handedly the reason she got on that show. She even went as far to ask me, "Do you want me to record it right now and put it on social media? It was all you!" In this circumstance, I was able to clear the air and let her know how hard those times were for me and how she could have changed that by simply taking the time to meet me for a coffee. She owned it. She was genuine and agreed that she didn't handle the situation right. That was all I needed to hear to move forward. Holding onto negativity wasn't an act of being my own best friend; instead, I saw her desire to make things right and now we have since become friends.

The expression that life can change on a dime rings true for me. I was offered the opportunity to become a regular lifestyle expert on the popular news program, *Inside Edition*. The person that connected the dots to facilitate this was at the assistant level at the time. He informed his colleagues at the show that I was already approved by their legal department, having appeared as a guest previously. He completely streamlined and fast-tracked the process on my behalf. Our first encounter was at a joint birthday party for two of our power publicist friends. It's not always the highest-ranking person with the power—it is the hard worker that pays attention.

I cherish this connection and have such admiration and respect for my friend, who has since advanced to a high-ranking producer in the television industry. The funniest part about the appearance that earned me placement was that it was a fashion show based on animated character themed bathing suits, which happened to be one of the highest rated segments for the show.

Being your own best friend **consists of getting creative** and putting yourself out there because you have to believe in yourself before anybody else will believe in you. If you want to work in a competitive industry where there are not many positions, you have to get creative. Seek out informational interviews or meetings whenever you have the chance. That's exactly what I did when making cold calls to public relations firms prior to graduating college, and being proactive yielded a positive outcome. You might not see immediate results, but this will open up doors for you when the time is right. Who is your dream company going to hire: the person who sent the cold email and résumé they receive from an address they don't recognize, or someone they met face-to-face and who went the extra mile to wow them? This is why making new connections is so imperative. You might have heard the expression "It's all about who you know," so go out and get to know people.

That's exactly how I know that paying attention to who is in the room is so important. While attending the opening of a Greek restaurant in Manhattan's Tribeca neighborhood, I noticed Bevy Smith. Influencer dinners were becoming popular, and as a person who prides herself on congratulating others that have made strides in this competitive business, I felt compelled to say hello. A couple of years later, we had the opportunity to work together creatively, when she was cohosting *Page Six TV* and I was cast as a lifestyle expert. The world can be a very small place, and typically that is the case, regardless of which industry you work in. If I didn't say hello when I had the chance, it would have taken a few more years to foster a friendship that we both might have missed out on.

What inspires your creativity? Tell me about your creative process.

Bevy Smith: "Daring to dream and having the time and space to do it, that's crucial to creativity! I start my days slow: prayer, journaling, taking a bath, having a good nutritious breakfast, taking my time before I get into the outside world. That gives me the room to just be, to set intentions and to manifest what I want my day to be!"

Val's thoughts: "Like Bevy, I dare to dream and have been doing so since I was a little girl. Slowing down can be challenging for me at times and is something I work on regularly, since it's an important part of my well-being."

...

Adam Weitsman: "Just because I don't want my life to be monotonous and I want to keep things creative and fresh. I listen to people's ideas and concepts and then follow those through with research."

Val's thoughts: "Like Adam, I love hearing from others that have new ideas and embrace brainstorming with them in effort to put them in motion. In fact, Adam is so giving with his time, it inspires me to want to help others further creatively."

...

Dale Moss: "I think I'm just curious and also absorb my surroundings very heavily. I've always felt as if I see things in a different way and that I can connect the dots in an abnormal manner. My brain is always going, and I guess I'm just comfortable letting it explore and dream."

Val's thoughts: "Dale is the first person to pat me on the back after each and every accomplishment. Whenever I am around him, his vibrant aura fuels me with excitement to use on new projects."

...

Ty Hunter: "My creativity is sparked by a blend of influences—music, art, culture, and the vibrant energy of the people around me. I find inspiration in everything, from the streets of New York to the latest fashion trends, and even in nature. The world is a canvas, and I love to soak in all its colors and textures. I also believe in allowing space for spontaneity. Sometimes the best ideas come when you're least expecting them—like during a walk or while listening to a great song. Embracing that organic flow helps keep my creativity fresh and alive.

Ultimately, it's about being open to inspiration from every corner of life and letting that guide the journey."

Val's thoughts: "Ty makes such a great point regarding the organic flow of creativity and how being open to it will enhance the process."

...

Countess Luann de Lesseps: "I am a creative person; it's just how I roll. I'm a busy body! I love to be productive. I tap in through the inspiration of others, and mentors that I'm so fortunate to have had."

Val's thoughts: "Luann is constantly building on her creative portfolio, going from reality star to international cabaret sensation selling out shows across the globe, and it's wildly inspiring to me."

...

Dr. Pimple Popper: "I like to think outside the box, so I'm always trying to think of ways to make things easier, less painful, less uncomfortable, faster, more efficient."

Val's thoughts: "Dr. Pimple Popper has such incredible bedside manner with her patients and I believe her effort to think out of the box has helped her there."

...

Vernon Davis: "I have always loved being creative and started painting at a young age. I was a studio art major at the University of Maryland (Go Terps!) When I was at the San Francisco 49ers, I started exploring acting classes and now I have done acting professionally. I truly just love the creative process and finding ways to tap into my creative side all the time."

Val's thoughts: "Vernon has many talents, so it doesn't surprise me how much he enjoys fostering his creativity in effort to master his craft."

...

Taylor Dayne: "Well, it changes overtime. When I was young, it was just a fire. It was like burning flames that I had to get out of Long Island. I had to get out of there and to do that I was using my greatest tool, my voice, as well as all the skills that I had to get into New York City and work with new artists. I pushed myself to know new bands, and constantly pushed myself so somebody would notice and I would get a record deal. The people in the room creatively inspired me. Now, it is sometimes silence that offers me inspiration. Nature is very inspiring for me, because what takes over when you become a big pop star is that you suddenly don't have that time of silence which helps you once again get creative. To be productive creatively, you must sit back sometimes. One must read and collect data, and to be completely inspired for me visually and sonically, hearing birds, nature, silence, and the clarity of it simplifies things for me.

It brings me a formal grounded feeling and that helps me want to feel like I'm open enough in my heart to be creative."

Val's thoughts: "Taylor truly practices what she preaches. I have spent time with her in nature and she is deliberate about using all of her senses to absorb what's around her. When we took a walk on her favorite beach in Santa Barbara, we dug our feet in the sand, listened to the waves, and walked with purpose in such a peaceful setting."

Being your own best friend also consists of **keeping good notes**. Maintain every contact in your database and update it regularly so you can utilize the connections you make. When work related opportunities come up and you are on a tight deadline, this will be super helpful in facilitating and delivering what has been asked of you. When I book a last minute television segment I need to be able to source products, sometimes in an extremely short amount of time. If I have the right person to reach out to, it makes the task at hand a whole lot easier to complete. Once, I was able to secure seven sneaker trends on a tight deadline for a daytime television segment. Another lifestyle segment was offered to me on a Friday afternoon for a Monday live taping. Even though I had a short window to prepare, I saw the impossible as important, and made it happen due to my connections. Nick Cannon and his talk show audience were able to learn how celebrities treat their undereye circles as a result of me being able to move fast. Knowing who to reach out to in a short amount of time will make your life a whole lot easier, less stressful, and allow you to move forward on opportunities for yourself.

The follow-up can sometimes be tricky. Several media executives have expressed to me that it is important not to inundate potential employers with messages. Instead, touching base just enough, coupled with quality information, will grab their attention. A great time to reach out is when you have a new project update that you place value on and can share. Be sure to research what the potential employer has been working on so your potential collaboration makes sense. What if you haven't received a response back? Don't overthink it; I have been in this position plenty of times. In that case, I recommend sending another email a couple weeks later. If you still haven't received a response, try again. Advocating for yourself can never hurt. Not receiving an answer is the worst that can happen, and then you can explore other options.

Standing out when it comes to new encounters is another fantastic opportunity you should seize. If you are invited to a small gathering where you think networking might make sense from a business perspective, be aware of who is in the room. Ask the host about the guest list in advance so you can kindly introduce yourself and effortlessly join their conversation without being pushy. Remember, being a good listener is a great way to deepen the initial connection. Find things you have in common. Be a good listener and complimentary in an effort to stay in touch. A smile and eye contact can create more good than you can ever imagine.

For me, when I reach my goals, my body experiences a high-intensity flow of energy. You could equate it with revving the engine of a sports car. These accomplishments VALidate me and my capabilities. This is one way that I know I am where I am supposed to be. Think about this concept for yourself: "Are you where you belong?" Once you figure that out, confidence and connections are the puzzle pieces that will come together and allow you to arrive and make an entrance when you do!

VAL'S EVALUATION: "BE YOUR OWN BEST FRIEND"

Creating a list of thoughts on how you can be your own best friend is an excellent tool to remind yourself what works for you. For me, this is always a work in progress, but there are some that remain constant. My list includes: learning from my mistakes and not beating myself up over them, practicing self-care in an effort to feel strong emotionally and physically, and not being afraid to explore new opportunities. This positions me to feel the most confident throughout my day and can be beneficial for you as well.

CHAPTER THREE

CELEBRITY KEYS TO CONFIDENCE AND CONNECTIONS

Why is being confident and developing meaningful connections so important? Feeling confident is empowering and people around you can sense your positive aura and want to be a part of that. When you emit this energy into the air, the people you come across are more likely to receive your efforts and a domino effect will occur. Being kind and sincerely complimentary to those around you creates a high vibrational environment, resulting in happiness and mood boosts. Respect is felt when given in pretty much every scenario, and with it, you can add a dash of sparkle to someone's day. When you are open to making new connections, there is no limit in terms of amazing scenarios you can find yourself in. Sometimes the people you are reaching out to need it more than you realize.

In this chapter, you will learn to unlock your confidence as celebrities reveal how they have fostered theirs. By unlocking the keys to their confidence, you'll have encouragement and motivation to persevere. You are also about to be informed how to implement icebreakers organically so that engaging with new individuals in conversation doesn't seem forced. I like to refer to this as the "Art of Talking to Strangers," which is something that readers will absorb throughout the pages.

Can you discuss the importance of feeling confident and making connections?

Dr. Robi Ludwig: "Feeling self-confident means appreciating who you are and recognizing the value you bring to the world. When you have self-confidence, you are more likely to treat yourself and others well, achieve your goals, and reject those who don't deserve a place in your life. Making connections not only feels rewarding, but also opens up a world of possibilities and opportunities for both yourself and others."

Val's thoughts: "If someone doesn't genuinely want to see you shine then they don't belong in your sphere. It's important to eVALuate those you allow to access your life and, if they are bringing too much negativity, move on from the relationship. As for Dr. Robi's take on making new connections being rewarding, I am in complete agreement as you may have already guessed."

...

Adam Weitsman: "Connections are paramount to success in both life and business. We live in a

> world of billions of people, all of whom have their own unique journey, skill sets, advantages, and disadvantages. Meaningful connections are how I built not only my social media presence of eighteen million followers but also my companies. I personally respond to every message that is sent to me, feeling that if someone is taking the time to message me, then I am going to give them the respect of a response. This has paid dividends both in my personal life as well as business as I have made so many wonderful friends worldwide as a result of connecting."
>
> Val's thoughts: "Adam and I used social media to initially build on our friendship, so I know how effectively he utilizes the platform."

Let's acknowledge our strengths and use them to our advantage. Not everyone has the self-assurance to chat with movie star Chris Hemsworth like I did about my personal life at a press lunch for his *docuseries* on *National Geographic,* titled *Limitless.* However, the examples I am providing you with will help you recognize the importance of sharing personal experiences in an effort to relate to people. Expressing emotion is an excellent way to connect on a human level, which can help you develop deeper connections with people in powerful positions. Incorporating small actions into your normal everyday activities such as speaking to the stranger in the elevator, the person in front of you in line at the grocery store, or the individual sitting in the chair next to you at the nail salon can yield major benefits.

One of my dearest friends was the person in the pedicure chair next to me.

Can you weigh in on our friendship and how it began?

Taylor Dayne: "Our friendship came very easily because you were a young, dynamic, positive, and powerful woman when we met. You were starting out in your career in publicity. I think I've always treated every human being in my life the same way: truthfully, honestly and directly. I saw your beauty and that you wanted to hear my truth. You stayed in the room and if you didn't like it you would leave. You seem to stay and I love you."

...

Where does your confidence come from?

Taylor Dayne: "My confidence came from meeting my fears, because I had extreme anxiety and trauma as a very young child. Standing up to that anxiety day after day, trying to take that pain, and learn how to invest in myself is where my confidence came from."

Val's thoughts: "Facing fears head on isn't easy, but if anyone can inspire us to do it with grace, it's Taylor. Her strength and vulnerability are palpable."

...

Harry Carson: "I think I got my confidence from my coaches both in college and the NFL. I also learned to have confidence in myself when I stepped onto the field, as I was trying to measure up to the guys that I was playing with or playing against."

Val's thoughts: "Healthy competition can enhance your set of skills and push you further out of your comfort zone for the better. By associating the feeling of being uncomfortable with breaking barriers and leveling up, you will begin to relate to the feeling in a more positive way.

...

Adam Weitsman: "From going through hard times, having my back against the wall and not having a plan B at the time. Adversity can be a strong character and confidence builder."

Val's thoughts: "While you are going through difficult times, it can be hard to see the good. However, I'm so glad Adam paints the picture of the power of resilience and how it leads to confidence."

...

Bevy Smith: "My secret to my confidence has much to do with my community of Harlem. I was raised to be proudly Black and that pride has allowed me to navigate spaces where most folks don't look like me! My parents are the other key to my confidence, as they instilled a strong work ethic in me and a belief that I could do anything if I was willing to work toward it."

Val's thoughts: "Community fosters confidence."

...

Ty Hunter: "Confidence comes from a deep understanding of yourself and embracing your uniqueness. It's about knowing your worth and owning it, no matter what the world throws at you. I draw my confidence from my experiences, the challenges I've overcome, and the people who inspire me. Surrounding myself with positivity and creativity fuels that fire. It's not just about the outer appearance; it's about feeling grounded and authentic inside. When you believe in your vision and stay true to who you are, that confidence radiates and becomes a powerful force."

Val's thoughts: "Owning who you are and what makes you special is of the utmost importance."

...

Vernon Davis: "My confidence comes from not being fearful of trying new things, no matter what the outcome may be."

Val's thoughts: "Vernon is not worrying about the possibility of hearing the word 'no.' I believe that is a strong testament to his winning record in all categories of his life! Looking at his response to the key to his confidence drives me to stop questioning myself. We all want to achieve a winning record, so I am going to do my best to take the Vernon Davis play."

...

Julia Haart: "I always think of myself as a time traveler. I traveled from the 1800s to the twenty-first century and I survived, and if I could do that, then I could do anything. I was my own PR machine, designer, and CEO rolled into one woman. When I first left the community and started my shoe brand in 2012 I got into a fashion party at Art Basel. I heard someone whispering that Tommy Hilfiger was in the corner of the room. I got up my courage and with my little notebook and pen, walked over to him. I started asking him hundreds of questions, merchandising questions, factory questions. He could've brushed me off or walked away, but he didn't. He sat down with me for forty-five minutes and really helped me and gave me such good advice.

An amazing addendum to the story is that, in 2021, Tommy Hilfiger approached me to partner with me on my avatar division in Elite World Group. He had no idea that we had met all those years ago in 2012. Here it was, nine years later, and he was asking to partner with me! I told him that we had met before, and I shared the story to see if he remembered ever helping a total stranger, and of course he remembered it. He didn't recognize me at all because when I was at Art Basel, I was still wearing my wig. I asked him why he had sat down and helped a total stranger. He told me, 'Julia, you looked so determined and so passionate about what you were doing, I didn't have the heart to say 'no.'"

Val's thoughts: "Julia acted like her own best friend and advocated for herself by taking action in a world that was completely foreign to her, allowing her to create a life for herself that she values. Julia is brave and bold and doesn't let anything get in her way, which I deeply admire."

...

Paula Froelich: "Okay, that's a funny one to me, because half the time I forgot I have confidence. I think I started my career with a 'fake it till you make it' mindset and sometimes felt like a big fraud. Now that I feel like I have made it, however, I look back at certain things and I know I'm really good. I actually know what to do in this situation and I got this."

Val's thoughts: "'Fake it till you make it' could also be considered as navigating your life with conviction. It's necessary to take you places. Don't be naive and act like you know everything; however, be strong if you believe in something firmly while simultaneously being open to listening, learning, and growing."

...

Can you pinpoint a moment where you decided to talk to a stranger and had a positive or impactful result come from it?

Adam Weitsman: "I cannot pinpoint just one moment, as I often will talk to strangers, both around home as well as abroad. I have met so many new and interesting people, some of which I have helped and others who have helped me, all from speaking with strangers. I have found that some of the best and most worthwhile relationships I have built all started from that first introduction or conversation."

Val's thoughts: "'The Art of Talking to Strangers' is my specialty (as long as you are in a safe situation of course.) I'm thrilled that Adam is in alignment with all of the benefits it can provide. Offering a genuine compliment to break the ice, asking a question, sharing a smile, and finding common ground are all methods you can try to connect and perfect this art."

...

Dr. Pimple Popper: "I talk to strangers every day at work. It's funny: I'm really good at it at work, but I kinda suck at it in certain circumstances. I think with anyone who works in a field where you have to talk to 'strangers' every day, probably comes across the same dilemma. I have positive impactful results all the time when I talk to strangers or my patients—they teach me so much about life."

Val's thoughts: "The only way to get better is with practice and that also applies to breaking the ice with someone new."

...

You are always your beautifully authentic self on camera and in person. Where does your confidence come from, and what do you say to those that need some tough love or motivation to get moving?

Isaac Boots: "I had a very Dickensian childhood. My mother was sixteen when she had me and she worked multiple jobs to support us. My mother and my grandmother (affectionately named Gram) were ironically both Geminis, and together they represented that balance for me. My Gram taught me love and my mother taught me drive. Despite the intensity of my relationship with my mother, she never let me be lazy. She wanted me to do well in school and take care of myself, and this ultimately led me to take the risk to move to New York the day after high school with a one-way ticket and only forty dollars in my pocket. Anytime I hear that little voice telling me, 'Don't workout,' 'Push that off,' or 'Do it later,' I silence it and just do it. Confidence comes from experience and, rather than feel down about a tough experience, it can be the fuel that helps you succeed."

...

How do you go about making new connections and building them? Please discuss why making new connections is so important.

Adam Weitsman: "I use social media and I try to build organic relationships by never asking people for anything. New connections are so important because it is how to effectively grow a business."

Val's thoughts: "Adam has grown countless successful businesses, so taking his advice on the subject matter is a smart move."

...

Dr. Pimple Popper: "Who you know is so important. I think it's one of the main reasons we attend college—the connections you make are key. That being said, sometimes it's hard to do so, especially if you are an introvert, or just don't feel like it."

Val's thoughts: "Doing hard things yields great rewards."

...

Vernon Davis: "I make it a habit to make new connections wherever I go, whether it's at charity events, sporting games, or just in my daily routine. Making new connections is vital to create new opportunities. You never know how just even one connection can be the start of something big!"

Val's thoughts: "I love this because Vernon and I decided to say hello, we became friends, and now I can share his victorious outlook with all of you."

...

Julia Haart: "The way I make new connections is by attending events and connecting to communities of all different sorts and so what I find is that if you're open and friendly to everyone, you can have an incredible array of friends, who will support you in time of difficulty and help you and be there for you and hold your hand. Find your passion in life and meet like-minded people."

Val's thoughts: "Growth and new hobbies are an excellent way to meet new people you can connect with."

Member of my ***"Confidence Community"*** Rob Shuter loves to take meetings and hang out at his favorite Chelsea neighborhood eatery. While eating dinner, at another table he spotted a television executive that had just relocated from the West Coast. That is an evening I will never forget, since she subsequently became one of my closest friends, who has been by my side during my brightest days and darkest times. This friend has mentored and advocated for me paving the way for my first big national television appearance. I am grateful for having been exactly where I was supposed to be that night, since this new connection grew into a lifelong friendship.

You and your TORCH'D workouts became a phenomenon during the pandemic, raising millions for those that were hungry around the world, as well as motivating people to stay fit during that time. Tell us about this experience, your reflection on it, and how important connecting with your fans and followers has been for you.

Isaac Boots: "I have always operated on instinct, not a strategic plan. When I started TORCH'D, it was for me. Then eventually it became my business. When I started doing the livestreams, I did it for myself so I had some accountability to work out and take my mind off the fear and anxiety around what we were going through. After a week, I imagined what I would have done in the eighties, growing up on food stamps and relying on school meals, and I just wanted to help kids who I knew would not be getting that daily meal from school during the lockdown. I still meet people in my travels and when I go out that share what it meant to them to have somewhere to go every day and move and laugh and give back what they could. I am so deeply grateful to everyone who participated, and I always think about that time and how scared we were. I love making people laugh and helping them to get a great ass, and I will do that for the rest of my life because what you see is what you get with me."

Val's thoughts: "Isaac's instincts were spot on. His TORCH'D community is still going strong."

Here are three questions to think about surrounding doubt:

1. Have you ever paused on a project you had passion for?
2. Have you ever received push back because you were told you didn't have enough of an audience or start-up funds to reach your goals?
3. Have you ever felt awkward or intimidated in a room of power players because you didn't know anyone upon arrival?

If you can let go of the excuses you tell yourself, doubt or a low confidence level will no longer be your state of mind. I want to help you from pressing the break and procrastinating when it comes to living your best life. As you can see, regardless of your so-called success level, everyone (including my ***"Confidence Community"***) sometimes questions themselves and has to work toward harnessing their confidence. It's how you navigate these less than perfect situations that will allow you to rise to the top.

One of the most valuable lessons I learned, and want you all to let sink in as well, is to stop waiting on perfection or being afraid of doing something wrong, or facing rejection. The truth of the matter is we are in control of our accomplishments and a can-do attitude is the key ingredient needed to summon what you want in life. Confidence and connecting is the remainder of the recipe and how you will gain access to that mindset. Let's keep reading and learn how to unlock and sharpen these tools.

We have all received the short straw at one point or another; now, it's time to push forward and secure the long one.

Can you discuss why making new connections is so important to you and how you were so open to our friendship?

Jen Selter: "I'm all about energy. During COVID, I spent a lot of time healing, focusing on myself, and learning to truly enjoy my own company. Without any distractions like relationships, I discovered that my high, positive energy is something I value. When I meet new people, I can instantly sense if they match that energy. You either connect or you don't—and when you do, it's something special that you hold on to. That's exactly what happened when we met; you had the most positive uplifting energy!"

Val's thoughts: "It's true! I was immediately drawn to Jen's vibrant personality. It's like we shared our positive energy with each other from the moment we met."

...

What is the key to your confidence, and how do you recommend others harness their own?

Jen Selter: "Confidence comes from knowing who you are and embracing your authentic self. When you're a good person with a kind heart and have a strong sense of self-worth, you naturally know what you bring to the table. That self-assurance becomes the foundation of your confidence. My advice to others is to focus on personal growth, surround yourself with positivity, and stay grounded in what truly makes you happy. Confidence follows when you are aligned with your values and proud of the person you are."

Val's thoughts: "Jen authentically portrays who she is both on social media and in everyday life. Authenticity shines through."

...

Can you please share your take on our initial encounter?

Julia Haart: "Val and I became friends because Val took the initiative at a party and walked over and introduced herself, and she has been a sister to me ever since. You really know who your friends are when your life falls apart, and Val was there every single day, holding my hand, being my friend. Val lives what she preaches and is sunshine in a human being. I think she's one of the most positive, inspiring, hardworking and determined people I've ever met."

Val's thoughts: "Hearing that from a woman who (other than my mother) is the most inspiring and strongest person I know knocked me off of my feet."

...

Can you share additional thoughts on the subject of connecting and confidence you feel passionate about?

Ty Hunter: "Connecting with others is at the heart of everything we do, especially in the world of fashion. Confidence isn't just about how we present ourselves; it's also about the relationships we build. When we engage authentically with others, we create a community that fosters support and inspiration."

Val's thoughts: "I love how Ty sums up his outlook on connecting."

Making people around you feel VALued is a huge part of how you can help connect with others and improve both your and their confidence. Sometimes, it's with an audience that might not come to mind right away. I know how special my mom felt when the organization she joined, which is a community for senior citizens to make friends and do social activities together, asked her to bring me on as an expert guest speaker for their platform that features well-known high profile professionals and celebrities. The members of the group were so engaged and interested in learning what goes into my profession as a lifestyle expert. It seemed that this was such a new topic and profession they were unfamiliar with and I think that's why it was of such interest. Having all of the different questions presented to me let me realize that I made them feel seen.

This was an extremely fulfilling experience and one that will remain as a standout. Everyone felt valued and that is all the takeaway I could ever ask for. After the presentation was completed, I had follow-up questions from different senior members asking me what skincare products I recommend. I loved being able to connect and share my knowledge, expertise, and recommendations on the topic. I also believe this helped my mom feel more comfortable meeting new friends in the group. She was happy I could provide my time which, in turn, made me feel good about helping.

I was passing through the farmers market in Union Square in NYC and I spotted Paula Froelich. While I had only seen her in person a handful of times, I took the minimal risk of embarrassment to catch up to someone who was technically a stranger to me. Even though I took her slightly by surprise, she was totally open to meeting me after I told her where I had begun my career and how I knew who she was. In fact, because I had so much respect for her and knowledge about her career accomplishments and insight into the contact she had with my former colleagues, we exchanged phone numbers on the spot and she revealed she was moving to Chicago and was not looking forward to it. As a natural born connector, my immediate thought was to link Paula with my friend who owns her own boutique public relations firm out of Chicago. What ended up happening was that my friend took Paula under her wing, including her without hesitation into her social circle.

From a connecting standpoint, what did you do to prepare for your move?

Paula Froelich: "I do remember that you saved my life. When I moved to Chicago, I sent out an SOS telling everyone on social media, 'Hey, I'm moving to the city that I've been to like once in my life, who knows anyone there who I can say hi to,' you were one of the only ones that really reached out and your friend became my rock during my two years in Chicago. So then I remember actually meeting you when I moved back to New York, and saying 'Thank you, thank you, thank you, I'll help with whatever you need."

Val's thoughts: "I'm just so glad I could help and make such a difference in someone's life by connecting them to another. In most industries (media and entertainment, especially), all worlds collide and lots of people know each other. It turns out that Paula and I have a wonderful mutual friend group and our hangouts are epic."

Let's move on to my firehouse friendship. One of the incredible perks I enjoy as a lifestyle expert is testing and trying out product after product. Everything from beauty to kitchenware, household appliances, jewelry, wellness products, and just consumer goods in general. I was collecting faster than I could clean out my closet, and brand-new unboxed items were swallowing my living room whole.

Whenever my mom comes to visit, we always make it a priority to straighten up and declutter. She and I have come to accept that I didn't inherit her exceptional organizational skills; let's just say that I am more the creative type. When she took a look at all of the appliances that had been sitting brand-new, in unopened boxes and hidden nooks and crannies of my apartment, she knew as much as I did that these air fryers, humidifiers, vacuum cleaners, packaged pillows, slippers, and so much more had to go. How many standing mixers and bedding sets can one bachelorette fit into her one bedroom New York City apartment?

This is when my mom and I had an aha moment! We were passing the fire station and that's when she said, "Wait a minute, let me just ring the bell and see if they take donations." We were greeted by a friendly firefighter who asked us if we needed assistance. He and the rest of his station were in for an amazing surprise. Over the past several years there have been many drop-off donations to the firehouse.

Now, the firefighters always make sure I get home safely. We watch the New York City Marathon together and have all become incredible friends. Because my mom went out of her way to make a connection with the firehouse, I now have an extended family. It's a wonderful feeling walking by every day, waving, saying hello and feeling welcome.

When one of the firefighters had an extra ticket to the Global Citizen Festival, he invited me along. This is when Hollywood's biggest stars come together in Central Park on a mission to end world hunger. We had access to the VIP tent and watched the headliner performers, like Mariah Carey, from the front of the stage. That night, I ran into a number of friends that I have worked with as well. This type of access to an event that was so high-profile all came from my connection and new-found friendship with my firefighter neighbors. I chatted with Jay Shetty, Nancy Pelosi, and Bevy Smith, the latter whom you know as a member of my ***"Confidence Community."***

VAL'S EVALUATION: "CELEBRITY KEYS TO CONFIDENCE AND CONNECTIONS"

By bringing to light my ***"Confidence Community,"*** and the methods they use to channel their inner confidence, my hope is that this has provided inspiration for you to do so for yourself. Your determination and spirit will be felt by those to whom you want to foster relationships with. Pushing yourself out of your comfort zone is vital to creating new opportunities, will knock down barriers, and unleash your confidence. New connections can open you to a whole world of positive energy and new friendships.

CHAPTER FOUR

DEVELOP YOUR SECRET FORMULA, BRINGING FORTH YOUR SUPERPOWER!

Our childhood memories have a lasting effect on our adult lives, some of which are not particularly pleasant to revisit. However, in doing so, we learn firsthand how to live with some of the not so easy ones. Childhood experiences have played a major role in who I am today. I'm a CONNECTOR! A person who wants people around her to feel their most confident! Where we come from or our so called circumstances, plus the personality traits that are passed down to us, are what make us unique.

Overcoming being bullied during my middle school years and feeling like an outsider turned me into someone who wants to make sure everyone feels included. Transforming my pain into purpose is very important to me. I choose to see my ability to do this as an innate gift. We all inherit qualities from our parents that help to shape our character, and my ease in connecting is something I learned from my father. Our personality incorporates all sides of ourselves, however we may only show a particular side depending on how we feel at the time based on how we choose to express our emotions.

As a young child and teen, I often felt embarrassed and judged. In terms of my upbringing, I came from two loving parents that financially had it far from easy. My mom worked as a preschool teacher and in office administration and my dad was a pest control technician and salesman. He fertilized lawns, was around chemicals regularly in the rigorous South Florida heat, and exterminated insects and bugs at other people's homes. Not once did I ever hear him complain about his circumstances. He suffered from mental health issues, information I was not privy to until my adult years, and that caused him to have habits and outbursts that were really uncomfortable to witness at times. One of his most embarrassing traits was that he hoarded junk he collected.

However, the other version of him is the man who will forever be my hero. A man of character who loved and cared for me and my brother more than any child could ever wish for. The man who instilled in me the belief that I could achieve anything I set out to accomplish. The man who would walk up to strangers and tell jokes followed by a belly full of laughter. He saw me as a true superstar, giving me the mojo I needed to make moves and never give up. That is who he was.

That was the side of him that sticks with me, his huge heart and the warmth he emitted as my biggest fan and cheerleader. I knew I could never stop fighting for my dreams. He always had my back and taught me the importance of loyalty and kindness. He was the kind of man who would drive hours in the night to take me to an *American Idol* audition; the kind of man who would hold my mom's purse while I performed Gloria Gaynor songs at the county fair because her back hurt; the kind of man who would allow me to take unconventional, one of a kind field trips, stemming from my outside of the box thinking as a teenager to interview celebrities during high school, since he believed it would further my life experiences, even when my mom would prefer me to go to class; and the kind of man who would do anything to keep his family safe and those around him smiling, laughing at his own corny one-liners. A memorable man who Pro Football Hall of Famer Harry Carson of the New York Giants remembers from the team practices my dad took me to as a toddler. Harry and I now regularly cross paths at philanthropic events and have since become friends.

Were you shocked that I was the daughter of that vocal fan from all those years ago?

Harry Carson: "Well, I wouldn't say that I was shocked when you identified yourself as your father's daughter because your dad left an impression, that every ball player at that time practicing and so forth, he sort of left his mark on because he didn't shut his mouth and just allow the coach to coach how they normally would. You never forget when you have a fan shouting out. That has always stayed with me from going to training camp. It's kind of a blah four or maybe five weeks, and then you have a distraction like your dad that creates a very memorable moment in time."

> Val's thoughts: "My dad had his flaws, but he always meant well. And now, because of him, my friend Harry Carson is taking the time to provide my readers with some inspiration. Thanks, Dad: our friendship has come full circle and is flourishing because of you."

Like most of us, I didn't have the advantages of coming from a connected family. Every relationship I developed and opportunity I achieved came from the courage my dad instilled in me. His gift was that he had no fear or worry about what others thought of him. His strong belief that his daughter had a sparkle to make magic happen on a greater scale without coming from connections or financial means resonated deeply. His legacy is the central reason it is important to me to help you unlock your superpowers and endless possibilities for greatness. Tapping into what makes us exceptional takes tenacity, and being able to hone in on what sets us apart and how we can affect people positively, can add light to our lives and to so many around us. My dad passed away, and even though he is not physically with me anymore, I will forever hold him and the resilience and confidence he taught me in my head and my heart.

My mom encouraged more traditional thinking and goals. She was grounded and the overall decision-maker of the household, with the exception of what my dad wouldn't bend on and so she sometimes had to admit defeat. She made sure I did well in school, had perfect attendance, and got to do the extracurriculars that were important to me and would look good on college applications, even though money was tight. She was present, loving and always put us first and truly was the most selfless mother. She dealt with mine and my brother's nonsense arguing over whose turn it was to be on the computer, or to sit in the front seat of the car, all while being the sole caregiver for her disabled father while she worked full-time. To this day, I still don't know how she managed to accomplish all this. Looking back, she truly deserves more than one gold medal.

Friday nights at the food court were a luxury for us, and when we made it to a restaurant, you could be sure we were carrying coupons. When I had sleepovers, I remember thinking if my friends used too much hot water my parents' electricity bill would go up. While my parents both made sure we never wanted for anything, internally I worried and sometimes questioned my capability, because the life I wanted for myself was going to be challenging to engineer, and my mom imparted a "play it safe" mentality. There were going to be lots of things out of my control, which always made me nervous, as well as a tremendous amount of uncertainty and sacrifices to make it happen for myself, but there was never any other way. I had to hustle, grind, and keep at it, despite the odds stacked against me in my effort to be happy and reach my potential in my profession.

Stress and anxiety have been something I have struggled with my entire life. Sometimes it feels so debilitating, but I still put in the work every day, like so many others in this world that have learned how to manage it since it never fully goes away. It's remarkable some of the moments in life we can remember so vividly from our adolescent years. I remember seeing a therapist just a handful of times when in middle school and her telling me to work on my breathing, as if that was going to make my bullies go away. While that was not the case, it did in fact equip me to calm my nerves and be less overwhelmed by the utter cruelty of the kids in my class. My parents did their very best, but my anxiousness had a way of overtaking me. At night, I was scared and had racing thoughts, which were terribly tough and sad at the same time.

I have always put pressure on myself to be as productive and perfect as possible. Even my fourth grade teacher told my mom, "You don't have to put pressure on Valerie, she will do it to herself, because she is an overachiever." Sixth grade was particularly difficult for me and I remember the cruelty of my classmates so clearly forever ingrained in my memory; perhaps this is partly why I find myself sometimes striving for external approval, even in my adult life. Therapists and psychologists I have spoken to constantly say that doing the hard work consists of opening your wounds from the past and sprinkling in some curiosity of how you got here can help you face your feelings and move forward.

In sixth grade, I stood in a parking lot just across the street from my home for hours, waiting to get picked up by the girl who I thought was part of the cool crowd. In reality, it was all a hoax. I ran home multiple times to call her and see why she was so delayed and she kept saying she was on her way. To my dismay she never showed. My eleven-year-old self didn't know it then, but that experience was gearing me up to grow into the confident person I am today. Whether it's emotional pain, an unpleasant situation, or feeling stuck, you can use these scenarios we find ourselves in as motivation to climb to the top. They can be turned into passion, purpose, and potential. Being on the ugly side of that situation allowed me to realize who I never wanted to be.

I turned into a go-getter as I reached high school and was pretty much a member of every social circle. I took on a role to make everyone feel included and I continue to do so today. Being left out and bullied left such a mark on me that I try to live everyday sharing upbeat energy with the world. I recognize character as the currency we should live by. Getting stood up and being treated like an outsider was a part of my growing pains, but I used the discomfort to shine bright and show myself and the world what I am made of.

This chapter is all about celebrating who we are and where we come from, regardless of our circumstances. Use them as fuel to conquer insecurity and hone in on your strength. It is important to note that not everyone around you will appreciate your shine and value, and that is okay, since it's not your job to convince them. Focusing on ways to discover who we are and where we really excel should be applauded.

Small offerings, such as treating the family in front of you with kindness, can have tremendous meaning and impact. Giving people who are dealt a challenging hand your compassion may remain in the person on the receiving end's heart for years to come.

I was recently visiting a theme park on a family trip. My mother, brother, and I were waiting to get on the studio tour ride. It was clear that the child in front of us was acting out and didn't have the patience to stay in line. I transported myself back to my camp counselor days and started talking to the child like he was one of my campers, trying to get him psyched for an activity he so obviously didn't want to wait to take part in. It was so clear his parents were relieved we were doing our best not to be disturbed by the child's tantrum. We smiled and conversed, speaking to him kindly, while trying to make him excited for the ride. At that moment, my mom looked at me and told me how proud she was of me. That moment brought me so much joy. My mother doesn't hand out compliments easily, and to witness how much my actions meant to her and the pride she had for me, tugged at my heart strings.

Treating people with kindness and connecting with them when they are going through difficult circumstances matters. It is most important that we value ourselves and reflect on moments and time periods in our lives where we have been responsible for affecting someone or a cause positively or made a difference. That young boy's father looked at me and revealed with a whisper that his child had special needs. His gaze and kind eyes said it all, how much compassion mattered especially in this moment. We replied, "He is so sweet and wonderful." Being understanding and connecting, even if it is for only a short amount of time, can have a huge impact and something we should always keep in mind.

A great way to open yourself up to taking a deep dive and learning further about yourself is to take into consideration how your friends and those closest to you would describe you. At my birthday celebration Julia Haart, a member of my ***"Confidence Community"*** suggested my friends go around the dinner table and reveal what they love most about me. Listening to those express how much they care and value our friendship for different reasons was eye-opening and heartwarming. Many of those in attendance at my party became acquainted through my personal introduction. Building these friendship bridges has been wonderful for all of us.

What are some ways that individuals can discover their strengths, and can you elaborate on the significance of this?

Dr. Robi Ludwig: "One exercise that I often recommend to my patients is to write down five things they know to be true and like about themselves. Additionally, I suggest asking someone who loves them to share five strengths they perceive my patient has. This exercise can help individuals identify their strengths, build self-awareness, boost confidence and self-esteem, and guide them in making choices that align with their abilities and values. Recognizing and leveraging one's strengths can lead to a more fulfilling, rewarding, and successful life."

Val's thoughts: "It was so important for me to include Dr. Robi's feedback on the subject matter due to her expertise and authoritative voice as a psychotherapist, and I love this strategy she has recommended."

We all have different personalities and qualities that make us unique. There is power in the way you package yourself, or being perceived a certain way based on your appearance. You want people to take notice of you for the right reasons and showing up with your head held high and conviction in your beliefs is a great way to gain respect. Consider your superpower synonymous with your it factor. Train yourself to recognize your strengths and really lean into them. Having identified and written about my superpower being a CONNECTOR, and how I came to recognize and nurture my superpower, the following are some of the golden nuggets I promised I would share earlier in the chapter from celebrities in my ***"Confidence Community."***

What is your superpower, how did you identify it, and how does it affect others positively?

Adam Weitsman: "I try to have strong leadership skills and I am a big proponent of building teams. I figured out later in life what people need to make them happy in the workplace and I've executed on those practices."

Val's thoughts: "Adam takes the time to meet the needs of his employees and people value that in a boss."

...

Julia Haart: "I think that my superpower is in the fact that I see the future instead of the present. I focus on the spaces in between; the products that the world should have but still doesn't. I don't care about accepted wisdom. I always try to find a way to do things better."

Val's thoughts: "It's this kind of thinking that makes Julia a disruptor and innovator."

...

Dr. Pimple Popper: "My bedside manner, my calm way that I speak to my patients. The way I can connect with my patients and make sure they trust me."

Val's thoughts: "As a bit of a hypochondriac, a good bedside manner puts me at ease when going to the doctor."

...

Vernon Davis: "I would say my superpower is manifesting. I am a firm believer that anyone can do anything they set their mind to. I truly love taking ideas from all different areas and turning them into reality."

Val's thoughts: "Manifesting works!"

...

Ty Hunter: "My superpower is the ability to connect with people on a deeper level and elevate their confidence through style and self-expression. I identified this power by paying attention to how I made others feel when I helped them curate their looks or share their stories. It's all about that transformative moment when someone sees themselves in a new light. To discover your own superpower, start by reflecting on what you're passionate about and what brings you joy. Think about the moments when you feel most alive and the skills that come naturally to you. Engage with others and observe the impact you have on them; sometimes, your superpower is revealed through the way you inspire or uplift those around you. Don't be afraid to experiment and explore different avenues—your superpower is waiting to be unleashed!"

Val's thoughts: "I know this is why Ty and I are friends, because I couldn't agree more with his beautiful outlook and the methods he suggests to discover and celebrate what makes you special by sharing it with others."

...

Countess Luann de Lesseps: "My superpower is energy. We all have a forcefield of energy; it's either positive or negative, and mine is positive. I bring positivity around me through my energy. If you have positive energy, you attract positive energy, it's as simple as that. I'm a big believer in meditation and manifestation: you manifest the life you want to live! If you put it out into the universe, anything is possible, but you have to believe it."

Val's thoughts: "Luann is in agreement with myself when it comes to manifestation being a powerful tool."

...

Dale Moss: "I've said this before, but my superpower is the ability to love and make people feel seen. I went through a lot of my life in a segregated community where I was judged because of the color of my skin and because our family didn't have a lot of money, so I know what it's like to be an 'outcast' and that's something I never want anyone to feel."

Val's thoughts: "Dale is an extremely warm person, so this makes absolute sense that he would identify his superpower as the above."

...

Rob Shuter: "I'd say my superpower is the ability to make people feel seen—like, really seen. It's something I've always gravitated toward, even as a kid. I'd be the one who noticed when someone was sitting by themselves, or when a friend said they were fine but didn't mean it. That instinct to tune into the emotions people hide under the surface is what eventually shaped my writing, too. I've always been drawn to the quiet, unspoken moments in relationships—the things we feel but don't always say out loud. I realized this was my superpower when I kept hearing the same thing from people, whether in life or through my writing: 'You put into words what I've been feeling but couldn't say.' It hit me that this ability to articulate the emotional undercurrent, to give voice to the things that scare us or make us feel alone, wasn't just a personal quirk—it was a gift. And when I leaned into it, everything clicked."

...

How does your superpower affect others positively?

Rob Shuter: "I think it helps people feel understood and less alone. When you see your experiences, your doubts, or your heartache reflected back at you, it's like a reminder that someone gets it. It creates a connection. In writing, it can be the difference between a good story and a meaningful one. In real life, it means that when someone's struggling or going through something they can't quite name, I'm there, helping them unpack it. It's not about giving advice or fixing things—it's about listening in a way that lets them know I'm with them in whatever they're feeling. This superpower of seeing and articulating the nuances of human experience builds trust, whether it's with readers or in personal relationships. It helps people open up, and sometimes, that's all we really need—someone to reflect back the truth of what we're going through so we don't feel so isolated in it. It's like holding up a mirror, but instead of showing them their flaws, I'm showing them their strength, their complexity, their worth."

What I'm finding as I reflect on the responses from my "Confidence Community" is that a lot of their beliefs are consistent. Countess Luann and Vernon talk about manifestation and Rob, Ty, and Dale allow people to be seen and have their own ways of doing so. Rob does it through writing, Ty through fashion and self-expression, and Dale transforming his childhood pain into purpose.

I consider my friend Jen Selter's superpower as the ability to influence, which is why I created the following question for her specifically.

How did you get started in the influencer space and what advice can you offer people following in your footsteps?

Jen Selter: "It's incredible to see how much the social media landscape has evolved since I first started. Back then, 'influencing' wasn't even a thing—I was simply looking for motivation and a way to connect with like-minded people around the world. My passion for photography and fitness, combined with working at a gym, naturally led me to share my journey online. What began as a personal passion turned into a career as I began receiving opportunities from brands I loved. I was juggling several jobs before fully committing to social media, and it's amazing to see how the industry has expanded across so many platforms today. My advice to those starting out is to remain authentic, stay consistent, and always align with brands or messages that reflect who you are. Authenticity is the key to longevity in this space."

Val's thoughts: "As Jen's friend, it's amazing to witness individuals in a room greet her with such excitement and appreciation for her content and

> opening the door for them to be able to create as influencers."

Finding a way to relate to new people and common ice breakers proves beneficial. One evening, I was having dinner at an Italian restaurant in Tribeca, planning a friend's baby shower with some girlfriends, all who happen to work in the public relations, media, and influencer space. There was no shortage of exciting conversation and lots of catching up.

When dinner was over and I was leaving the restaurant, I spotted two men in matching jackets with the logo for *The Equalizer* on them. It briefly dawned on me that they may have been coming from the set of the network primetime television show, which is one of my mom's favorites. I approached them and mentioned how much my mom enjoys the show and got the sense the men were related. My intuition was true as we continued chatting. My icebreaker was expressing that my mom is a fan of the show. As it turned out they were father and son and the father was actually the showrunner, who is literally in charge and runs the show. He couldn't have been more kind and humble and was so receptive to making this new relationship and connection with me. I was not shy in sharing the bond I have with my mother and expressed how happy I am when she joins me when I am working in studio. Our familial bonds and the importance that we had that in common shined through.

Since they were so nice and easy to talk to, I mentioned that if they ever have a role to fill as a news reporter, they could look no further because I would love to do it and have the appropriate credentials. Fast forward a year and a half later, after remaining in touch through multiple texts and following up just the right amount, and the opportunity presented itself.

As I was sitting at a skincare luncheon across from television writing legend, my friend Candace Bushnell, the original Carrie Bradshaw and creator of *Sex and the City*, the text I'd been waiting for all that time came through that there may be a role for me on *The Equalizer*. It was so invigorating to be able to share this news with her and she reciprocated my excitement.

A week later, I received a call from casting, and I submitted my self-tape audition within the hour, as the television industry moves fast and you always have to be ready. In fact, that is a good rule to follow, regardless of your industry, so always keep that in mind. Two days later, I received the offer and was cast to play a news anchor on the primetime show.

How random run-ins lead to new connections—While dining in an exclusive French restaurant in Sag Harbor in the Hamptons, I noticed television host Tamron Hall at the table next to me. We were seated on the deck and I was with a few girlfriends that I was traveling with for a weekend getaway. One of my dearest friends is a producer on Tamron's daytime talk show. During one of our conversations, he mentioned how he felt recognized and appreciated throughout the television season. Tamron had called him at the end of the season to personally thank him for doing an exceptional job producing.

This didn't come as a surprise to me since my friend is sharp, talented, and detail-oriented, as well as easy to work with. He produced me for a segment on *Good Morning Britain* in the past and it was a fantastic experience. The following morning, I was scheduled to appear on *Good Morning America* virtually to chat about entertainment content releases via Zoom.

My inner voice and thought process was trying to tell me that I should go over and introduce myself. Tamron was sitting at a table of about ten people when I made the snap decision to say hello and make her aware of our mutual relationship with her producer. During the conversation, I highlighted what he had shared with me and how much pride he took in her praise. Tamron completely embraced my hello and my pointing out that her gratitude made an impact on an integral part of her team. In general, being appreciated and acknowledged for hard work feels good and she was happy to hear how she affected my friend.

Fast forward a month later, and I was having brunch in the Meatpacking District in New York with my friend, celebrity fitness personality Isaac Boots (also a member of my ***"Confidence Community"***) and his husband. As we exited and headed onto the cobblestone street, and to my surprise, Tamron Hall was sitting at a table right in front of us. In my head, I was thinking, *What are the odds that the universe would bring us together again so quickly?* In my greeting, I said, "Hi Tamron, Valerie Greenberg, #youvebeenVALidated, we met in Sag Harbor, do you remember me? I am close friends with your producer." She did.

The next day, I received a call from my friend who is the producer on her show. He told me that he just got off of a team production meeting with Tamron. He continued to say, that during the team Zoom, Tamron told him, "I met someone you know, or at least, I think you know. She speaks so highly of you and was singing your praises."

Based on when I had initially mentioned approaching Tamron in the Hamptons to him, he answered her, "Oh, it must be my friend Valerie Greenberg."

Tamron replied, "Yes, that sounds right."

He also told me she said something to the effect of we all need a Val in our corner and he replied, "Well, Tamron, it seems to me that #youvebeenVALidated."

He said he and Tamron had a good laugh about it and I laughed as well when he told me the story.

It seems quite hilarious if you picture me, a random person approaching her with knowledge about her staff, when in all reality I could have been some crazy fan or stalker. However, in this situation, we all realized and appreciated that I was using my superpower as a connector.

The connection between myself and the show runs even a little bit deeper. During the SAG-AFTRA strike, it was no secret that actors and performers were looking for alternate ways to stay busy and fulfill their need for artistic work opportunities. Connecting the dots for others can have a tremendous impact and be great for people you care about in your life.

My friend Leon is a sensational actor, whose credits include *Cool Runnings*, *The Five Heartbeats*, and even Jesus in the iconic Madonna "Like A Prayer" music video. We initially met at a premiere for 50 Cent's hit series *Power*, and he was just the nicest guy. We continued to have random run-ins at events and would trade supportive messages on Instagram to each other, which led to us becoming friends. He was kind enough to be one of the first guests on my podcast, *The AV Effect*, that I co-host with Emmy Award-winning journalist Alicia Quarles.

When Tamron's producer listened to the episode with Leon as our featured guest, he thought Leon would be an excellent guest for *Tamron Hall*. Leon had previously invited me and a plus one to a performance of his band Leon & the Peoples.

My producer friend accompanied me and I introduced him to Leon. By connecting my producer friend and Leon's talent rep, a few weeks later Leon was a guest on *Tamron Hall*, talking about career highlights and promoting his band's tour. This all came as a direct result of me making the connections.

VAL'S EVALUATION: "DEVELOP YOUR SECRET FORMULA, BRINGING FORTH YOUR SUPERPOWER!"

This chapter covered the influence our childhood and environment play in our development of our superpowers. Situations were highlighted where a snowball effect of connections and positive outcomes transpired for all parties involved through friends supporting and being open to creating opportunities for one another. Reflecting on what makes us special and using our superpowers can set wonderful opportunities in motion. So, go out into the world, and show everyone your superpower!

CHAPTER FIVE

TENACITY TALKS

To me tenacity means persistence, determination and perseverance. My personal motto is plain and simple: keep going and don't stop. There are countless successful people who didn't allow their negative experiences of not acquiring their dream job, having their business plan turned down, or weren't selected for a role they auditioned for and desperately wanted discourage them. You may begin to think, "Why not me?" We all get up in the morning, brush our teeth, wash our face, and have the same basic needs as humans. The only person that can stand in your way of taking care of yourself is you. You have the power to keep yourself going. You need to remember that you are capable and not inflict limitations on yourself. There are many reasons why you might not have been selected and any one of them may not have been directly related to your performance.

Mantras are a method that are helpful for me when I want to push myself a little further and reframe my thoughts. When I'm running or in the middle of a tough workout, I cheer myself on by saying, "Go, Valerie, go, there are no limits," over and over, and before I know it, the workout is complete and I ran the extra mile. It may sound simple, but it truly works. My curiosity as to how tenacity has played a role in the lives of my ***"Confidence Community"*** is important for me to share with you.

Tell me how being tenacious has helped you reach your goals.

Adam Weitsman: "There is no choice when your back is against the wall and you have obligations, you have to do what you need to do in order to come through for the people relying on you."

Val's thoughts: "I am very much in agreement with Adam on this."

...

Can you please reveal something about yourself that most wouldn't know about you with regards to your tenacity?

Dr. Pimple Popper: "I don't really say 'no' to many asks of me, and this could maybe be my eventual downfall, because I probably take on more than I should, but I think this commitment and the hard work that I have put in has put me where I am."

Val's thoughts: "It is important to check in with your friends and ask them how they are doing since having lots of commitments can sometimes be overwhelming."

Merriam-Webster dictionary defines passion as "a strong liking or desire for or devotion to some activity, object, or concept."[1] If you really think about this for a moment, and focus on what you are passionate about, you'll feel happy and content. We already dove into developing your technique for positivity (which was also referred to as your superpower) in the previous chapter. Once you have identified your unique special qualities and talents, you will have clarity on your strengths. You're in possession of the information you need which will serve you in a tremendous fashion while pursuing your passion. Living and breathing your authentic happiness allows you to lean into your natural attributes and your truth, helping all of the uncontrolled variables in this world to align.

The ability to live your life loving what you do, around people that challenge you and help you grow on a daily basis, is a privilege and takes hard work and determination. This is where tenacity comes into play and why it is so important to highlight. If you live tenaciously, only you can get in the way of your goals and your purpose. Through your life experiences, you will find yourself in social dynamics where you will come across opportunities to create more relationships. When you have access to exceptional people, do not allow the moment to pass you by. You will come to realize, as you incorporate what you are learning throughout these chapters, that some of the most influential people will respect you for your bold, vibrant energy and putting yourself out there by saying hello and just

1 Merriam-Webster.com Dictionary, s.v. "passion," accessed September 29, 2024, https://www.merriam-webster.com/dictionary/passion.

being who you are. You'll also see that they themselves practice tenacity.

When my professional career first began, I had the opportunity to interview powerful people and celebrities. Internally, my body recognized my nerves and anxiety; however, I was aware that focusing on those emotions wouldn't get me anywhere. Utilizing my drive and passion helped me overcome those questionable feelings and led me to the moments where I would be acknowledged and embraced by those I was speaking to. As my skills strengthened, it increased my ability to foster friendships with elite people in all facets of the business and entertainment world.

There is one movie star who I keep randomly running into. Achieving his level of blockbuster fame takes hard work and tenacity. What stands out to me about this individual is how he maintains an extremely humble demeanor while being such a box office success.

The first time I met Glen Powell, I was mourning a breakup at a private members club, when I spotted him, smiled, and waved in his direction. Clearly, my confidence shined through, since he walked over to me and asked if we had met before. This encounter was prior to the release of *Top Gun: Maverick* and my assumption was that he just happened to be a good-looking guy, not one of the biggest up and coming movie stars.

A year later, we recognized each other when we were dining at the same restaurant. He walked over to my table and met my mom, and we exchanged phone numbers. A little more than another year later, when I was visiting Los Angeles, we almost bumped into each other as he was entering the door that I was exiting from at the hotel we were both staying at.

Glen's interaction with me on multiple occasions demonstrates the value he bestows upon our friendship that was built on fate, and I believe the reason for this is I exude a genuine, friendly, and confident aura. You never know who you will meet and when they may pop into your life, so portraying a confident, sincere manner, combined with tenacious behavior, will be appreciated and well received. My hope is that we will come across each other again, in business or personal settings, and that Glen Powell will have those same positive feelings toward me.

Preparation is key for feeling confident when you are going to be in a situation where you want to leave an impression on someone. An important tool to utilize is visualization. Merriam Webster defines this as formation of mental visual images. By practicing, it will gradually become easier to change your social behavior and it will become second nature to you; think of it as a dress rehearsal so you will be polished and ready when unplanned encounters appear. You will start to take notice of how your efforts will help you build strong relationships with those you desire to connect with. So many of my relationships, including my ***"Confidence Community,"*** developed through genuinely wanting to learn more about the people I respect and admire.

As a natural born extrovert, considering myself effortlessly outgoing, cultivating conversations with new people comes naturally to me, as I am pretty sure you have recognized. However, you can be just as determined and passionate if you are an ambivert, (which is defined by Merriam-Webster as a person who has characteristics of both an introvert and an extrovert) or an introvert, but it just might take a little more practice. Try to train yourself to associate a positive feeling with social anxiety if you happen to experience it, as this will allow you to conquer your discomfort and will be beneficial to you. Recruit a friend to practice this exercise with you, since making yourself vulnerable will help you learn new skills and being open to growth will enhance your ability to communicate effectively.

Sometimes, you have to make sacrifices in order to get to where you want in life. There were plenty of times I couldn't afford to fly home for the holidays and that was heartbreaking for me and my family. When I had to cut corners by eating ninety-nine cent pizza, I would sometimes get frustrated that I wasn't able to eat nutritiously. My journey also consisted of living with roommates in order to make it financially feasible to make a home for myself, something that is quite common in big cities. During my apartment search, I took an untraditional approach to finding a place to live: using my skills as a connector, I mentioned my search to the manager of a popular nightclub Tenjune. Lucky for me, he had a friend who was looking for a roommate, which led me to an apartment I would call home for several years.

At first, this was a great scenario and I can honestly say I am so grateful for where I ended up. There are just a few situations that were less than ideal that I found myself in. This is where my perseverance was imperative to lean into.

There was one predicament where someone posing as a teacher never turned in their paperwork to become a legal occupant by the deadline. That raised some red flags right out of the gate. When I let this person know that this was a deal breaker for me, they left—but not quietly. They ended up throwing a fit, making false claims, stalking me, inundating me with frightening prank calls, and I had to get the authorities involved.

Another situation involved a girl who had a foul odor coming from her bedroom that was permeating into the hallway. The scene in her living space was atrocious: her drawers were open with half-eaten, weeks-old nacho remnants on my dishes. It was a shock to see unfinished salad bowls with my silverware encrusted with her food under her bed. This girl admitted to me that she was engaging in self-destructive behavior, which was quite evident from what I witnessed. Not knowing those close to her personally, I reached out to her family via social media to let them know the gravity of their daughter's depression.

In another horrible circumstance, a roommate moved her boyfriend in and tried to put it past me without paying any extra rent. It's hard for me to be shocked as to what people are capable of anymore after these experiences. Needless to say, I am so glad the roommate chapter of my life is closed and these types of sacrifices are behind me. My determination got me through these hard times and I did not waver or give up by settling. There was even a time when an investigator called my childhood home in effort to obtain information on one of my roommates, who was the sister- in-law of a media personality who is now inarguably one of the most famous women in the world.

Moving into my own apartment marked a significant time in my life, and one I am so grateful for. To me, it symbolized how far I've come after all of the challenging times I faced when living with so many different people. There were, of course, some terrific roommates, and that is the positive I choose to take away from living with a vast array of people, the lifelong friendship I gained with my last roommate. My initial connection with the Tenjune club manager led me to a friend who I lived with throughout the pandemic and who has since truly become family. We could always (and continue to be able to) count on each other, and we have also inspired each other creatively.

Other persistent behavior I've exhibited includes a social experiment where I walked around New York City asking people to follow me on Instagram. My reasoning for this is that as a creative, the number of followers you have and social media presence can be an influential factor in business dealings. Testing out new techniques to increase my following was an experiment I embraced. Being honest and open to asking people for the follow was a challenge I faced head on and I received 100 new engaged followers on that day. This experience did allow me to grow as a person and recognize how honesty resonated with people along with my original content.

Keep in mind, putting in the effort will **Turn "No's" to Nods**. Noting the value of under promising and over delivering is vital. Here are some suggestions below on how you can set yourself up to win.

As a businesswoman, I have cultivated relationships with various CEOs and decision makers and sometimes, when presenting new opportunities to collaborate, the initial response back to me was a pass. This is when I figured out how to turn their horizontal headshake into a vertical one. Balance is the magic word: sweeten the pot for your potential client by adding extra value to your initial proposal. Keeping an open mind when it comes to compromise and negotiation is important. As long as your value is still intact, both parties can benefit.

Understanding that nurturing and relationship building takes time and the deal might not immediately get done. Wherever you are located geographically, whether it be a small town or a big city, you can make these tools work in your favor, getting you closer to what you want to achieve.

Have you turned "No's" to Nods?

Adam Weitsman: "A lot of times, but it has to be with your conviction and you have to back it up with fact, not just opinion."

Val's thoughts: "If you can offer proof of concept, this will be helpful in securing a vertical headshake."

Based on the authenticity of my own brand #youvebeenVALidated, media professionals, acquaintances, and people I don't even know are reaching out regularly to me to make a connection for them. Their requests can range from setting up an introduction to a particular person; asking to have me endorse or promote their products; connect them for a business venture; or inviting me and a guest to their dinner party or special event. As a direct result of my hard work, this wide range of people view me as an agent without the official title, responsible for facilitating many successful opportunities for people, because I'm someone who connects the dots. I refer to myself as the liaison between every other expert in most industries.

Whether I have a colleague that is looking for a shooting location or a friend that is casting for a certain project, I am constantly connecting them and am happy to do so. I also think about the times when helping someone else worked to my benefit.

My first appearance on a New York television morning show stemmed from including a former colleague's client in a segment I presented on a Baltimore morning television show, and several months later I was top of her mind when she linked me with her producer friend who needed an entertainment expert to chime in. It's a two-way street, and true friends acknowledge and reciprocate when they can.

My determination and openness have afforded me a seat at the table, since I have unlocked many doors with my positive attitude and enthusiasm. "Don't be afraid" and "never give up" are phrases that continue to guide me through my life's journey. My constant hustle is noticed, and those around me recognize that I truly treat everyone with the same respect and friendliness, whether you are the handyman in my building or the CEO of a large company.

My handyman has always made himself available to me with a smile, and he and I have cultivated a friendship. I've been able to gift his wife and children with items I have received, as a thank you for his hard work. When he went to Nepal with his family, he returned with matching pashmina shawls for both my mother and me. Then, I have friends with estates who generously invite me with a guest to their intimate, curated dinner parties. All of these relationships are of equal importance to me.

When I witness those around me being courteous and kind to others, I can't help but smile. When visiting family, my brother answered the door and a lovely exterminator walked in during the dog days of summer. She had such a wonderful energy about her. My brother immediately offered her a bottle of water or Gatorade, to which she replied, "Wow, you have no idea how many people barely acknowledge me, let alone offer me water or refreshments." Being there in that moment and seeing how in tune my brother and I are with treating others thoughtfully was wonderful. There is no gesture too small when it comes to kindness and affecting others positively when connecting.

Getting to the point where I am able to spread my message #youvebeenVALidaed on a greater scale feels incredible. As I mentioned, relationship building takes time and reaching certain heights doesn't happen overnight. An audition I had submitted for through a talent executive received a response, but I ultimately wasn't selected. At the time I didn't have an existing relationship with this person, however, she remembered me, noting that I remained in contact with her 'Just enough,' as she put it. Through trial and error I learned where to set limits so that I didn't become bothersome. Even though I didn't get the initial role, my reaching out and not giving up allowed the executive and I to become further acquainted with one another. She then advocated for me as she got to know me through my friendly persistent behavior. Remaining ready, prepared, and putting in the work allowed me to be successful when a new opportunity presented itself for *Page Six TV*, and I became their lifestyle expert.

Sometimes, you are being observed and you don't even realize the influence you have. In one case the person was my brother, and I didn't realize the positive impact I had on him. While in high school, he wrote an essay advocating for himself to be grandfathered into a program that was ending, but he had earned his spot. He had seen me in action advocating for myself to create opportunities for me in high school, which led him to try and do the same for himself. Don't let others who hold a little bit of power get you down. Let your voice be heard when you believe strongly in something. In his case, it worked out, and he was able to get a parking spot he was promised, that the school tried to renege on. This is a moment in his teenage years that helped him see me in a new light as his big sister.

When I first moved to New York, I knew I had to prove myself as a freelance reporter to my magazine editor. The assignment was to interview Paris Hilton, who at the time was expanding her empire, and adding DJ and pop star to her list of credentials. While most of the reporters got tired of waiting outside, I didn't leave until I convinced the publicist of the venue to provide me access. My credentials were only for the red carpet portion, but since Paris was running late, she wasn't able to chat with print reporters. As I made my way inside, I introduced myself to Kathy Hilton and uncovered Paris' childhood nickname from her, acquiring good quotes I could share with my editor. My determination and perseverance were respected.

On my journey of determination, I developed and created a short form series concept for a magazine's digital platform called "Crosstown Connections." Standing out in the rain and asking random strangers if we could take a ride together in an Uber Pool in order to get to know someone new was part of this process. There was little financial backing and resources, but this challenge served a purpose in both my personal and professional growth. The premise, consistent with my passion for connecting, was the theme throughout the series. Putting my ego aside and filming on my smart phone, with an intern handling all production (under my guidance) was how we were able to complete it. Having my own project and being creative kept me busy and focused at slower moments. While the series only lasted one season, I chose to take away what I learned and the brand partnerships I secured as a win.

My career has blossomed and continues to do so through my positive outlook and resistance to negativity. Some of my television credits include: guest correspondent on *E! News*; MorningSave lifestyle Expert on *Extra*, *Inside Edition* and *The Steve Wilkos Show*; and entertainment and lifestyle expert on *Good Morning America*. With my no limits mentality, I am expanding into the literary arena, writing this book, as well as being a columnist for *Hamptons Storyboard* magazine. My acting credits include the Max series *And Just Like That…*, as well as CBS' *The Equalizer*. My credits also span internationally, reaching Germany on their biggest network RTL as a society expert on its programs *RTL Exclusiv* and *Guten Morgen Deutschland*.

It is a privilege to be able to share my entertainment and lifestyle expertise with a broad audience. However, as you have been reading, it has taken me time to get to where I am. Learning to exude confidence, believe in myself, talk to strangers with ease, make the most of my very best qualities, and not obsess over what makes me feel insecure at times can be challenging! Providing you with the secrets that helped both me and my ***"Confidence Community"*** push through, you can now use as your own and make them work for you.

The roster of interviews I've conducted with Hollywood heavyweights for *E! News* include: Ryan Seacrest, Mark Wahlberg, Rita Moreno, Priyanka Chopra Jonas and Jennifer Hudson. My experience, determination and handling challenges gracefully got me here. At the Tony Awards, upon my first days reporting for *Us Weekly*, I was able to have Oprah answer my question and the reason being, she clicked with my delivery and enthusiasm. She stopped, and addressed me on the red carpet specifically, despite the fact that the show was about to begin. The doors were literally closing and security was attempting to rush her in, but it turned out she would make time for me before making her grand entrance.

My commitment to inspire, connect people, and uplift their confidence is what brings me joy and never wavers. One of my mottos is "have no fear and you will persevere." "Don't Be Afraid," has a lot of significance for me, as it was born out of the title of a song that I wrote and recorded in high school.

Here is the first line of my original song and a philosophy that remains constant in my life: "I can do anything as long as I have faith in my dreams."

Having a bubbly, outgoing, and energetic personality might make me appear carefree at times, but the reality is that I am a perfectionist and there are plenty of moments where my nerves try to get the best of me. What puts me at an advantage is that I have made a deal with myself that I will not give up and will meet these challenges, not push them away. For you, what will help is asking yourself why these nerves surface when they come up. Use these uncomfortable feelings to work to your advantage every time you pick up the phone to follow up on a pitch, take action to secure a new client, or whatever your task may be. Once you make initial contact, the relationship will begin to develop and flourish, as will your comfort level and confidence.

Connecting has always been a part of who I am. In high school, I convinced my vice principal to make my *MTV Spring Break* vacation in Key West a television production field trip specifically created for me. Having perfect attendance in high school was my goal and I didn't want to forgo the $500 award that came with that accolade. To paint the picture for you, my senior year was coming to a close and I firmly believed these life experiences and connections to be cultivated would be impactful for my future career. Ashton Kutcher and Gabrielle Union were some of the talent participating in the productions I was invited to be a part of. My thought process was that as a senior television production student, shouldn't being on MTV be synonymous with going to class? I ended the year without an absentee mark on my record and got to keep my VALidated parking spot and the money I earned by this accomplishment.

That wasn't the first time I received permission to create a unique field trip. While in high school working for Radio Disney, the opportunity to interview Boy Band BBMak presented itself. To this day, my mom remembers receiving a phone call from my vice principal asking her permission if it was okay for him to allow me to miss school and conduct this interview. She said yes, and my friend's mom drove us to Miami. What a fun, confidence building experience to remember.

Singing brings me so much joy. Throughout my elementary, middle, and high school years I would often land the solo as a natural-born performer. I'd competed in several talent competitions and was always known as the girl in the class with the great voice. This recognition from my peers was very important during my formative years. My song "Don't Be Afraid" is a theme that constantly resonates through my life as I previously mentioned and also served as Radio Disney theme music during my weekly Radio Disney show that I cohosted with my childhood best friend.

As a summer college intern, working at *Rolling Stone* magazine, I approached Jann Wenner, founder of *Rolling Stone* and chairman of Wenner Media, and I expressed enthusiasm for the opportunity and position. Being an intern is often associated with doing menial tasks, but by making myself known, I received invites to the celebrity luncheons the publisher would host in the office.

A few years ago I arrived at a cocktail party in support of a charity event a little bit early. The doors hadn't opened just yet and it was chilly out. There wasn't quite enough time to run an errand, so I waited patiently and decided to strike up a conversation with a woman who was also waiting. It turned out she was a television producer for an international TV network. Through that encounter, I received a decade of freelance work on German T.V, commenting as a society expert on breaking celebrity stories.

A few years later, German television enlisted me to create a really fun video package for one of their entertainment programs, about being a fabulous girl about town in New York City. My assignment was highlighting the *Sex And the City* reboot *And Just Like That….* Our first stop was Sarah Jessica Parker's shoe store, which at the time was very popular, and she was actually there working as a salesperson. My producer and I walked in and introduced ourselves. I remember how important I felt at that moment when she addressed me by name because I felt an instant connection created between us. One of my regular practices when I meet someone is to call them by their name. Everyone likes to be remembered and it makes them feel special. I try to look for a commonality between myself and the person I am meeting. SJP is a true business women who helped me find the perfect pair of shoes that day. Seeing her work ethic made her relatable and as a fellow business women I decided to thank her by revisiting the store to drop off my #youvebeenVALidated leggings as a gift. While I am on the topic of class act celebrities, Priyanka Chopra Jonas addressed me by my name during the interview I was conducting with her, and these simple moments with these actresses helped me learn the importance of treating others in this manner.

Can you tell me about the importance of tenacity?

Rob Shuter: "Tenacity has been everything for me. There was a time when I was juggling multiple freelance gigs, trying to make ends meet while also writing on the side. I'd wake up early, squeeze in some writing before the day job, then come home and keep going until my eyes couldn't stay open anymore. But I had this unwavering belief that if I kept showing up—if I didn't let rejection or exhaustion stop me—it would eventually pay off.

One of the most tenacious stretches of my life was when I was trying to break into writing full-time while working a demanding job. I remember writing in the early mornings, crammed into a tiny studio apartment where I had no real desk, just a table that doubled as a kitchen counter. I'd send out short stories and pitches to editors, and for every acceptance, there were ten rejections. It could've been easy to just stop, but there was something inside me that refused to quit. I was in a constant battle with doubt, but I kept going because the alternative—giving up—wasn't an option.

What got me through those years was this relentless commitment to the bigger picture. I knew I couldn't control how fast things happened, but I could control how much effort I put into it. I learned to see every small step as progress. Even when nothing seemed to be happening, I was building resilience. And that resilience, that refusal to quit, is what eventually led to bigger opportunities.

Now, when I look back, I realize that the tenacity wasn't just about reaching a goal; it was about becoming the kind of person who doesn't stop when things get hard. That mindset has helped me push through creative blocks, build meaningful connections, and keep writing when the doubt creeps in. The best part? That tenacity inspires others to see what's possible for them, too. When people see that you kept going, no matter the obstacles, they start to believe they can do it, too. It creates this ripple effect of resilience."

Val's thoughts: "Like Rob, I, too, have faced being questioned and it is not a good feeling, however, I preVAiL (I use this phrase as a reminder that I can accomplish anything by reminding myself that I have my tenacity and affirmations to lean on)."

...

Can you share examples of turning "No's" to Nods?

Dale Moss: "I've done that my whole life by being myself. People always think I'm a certain way until they know me and, honestly, I never stress about judgment. The greatest gift I received in a lot of ways was being judged early and often because I learned not to let it bother me!"

Val's thoughts: "We have to stop worrying about what other people think about us and join Dale and his thought process on not letting negative opinions affect our stride."

...

Countess Luann de Lesseps: "All the time! I was very gung ho on having Kelly Killoren Bensimon back on the Housewives, and then *The Real Housewives Ultimate Girls Trip: RHONY Legacy* came along. It's called the power of suggestion!"

Val's thoughts: "Luann lifts her girlfriends up, and I love this about her."

...

Vernon Davis: "I personally try to look at every opportunity in front of me and not take it for granted. Given that I started my young adult life in the sports industry, I took full advantage of the opportunities thrown my way. As I transitioned out of my sports career and dove into my other endeavors and acting career, I applied the same mindset."

Val's thoughts: "Taking action is a tenacious behavior."

...

Julia Haart: "I always say that in business, a no is a slow yes. To me, every time I've gone into an industry, I've been a disruptor and at first people don't understand what I'm doing, and they not only tell me, no,' they doubt it can be done, until I actually do it and prove them wrong."

Val's thoughts: "Go Julia, Glow Julia! Even if you take just a little piece of Julia's thought process, you are setting yourself up to win."

...

What challenges have you faced professionally and personally and what strategies have you used to overcome them?

Bevy Smith: "Changing my life at age thirty-nine, going from an advertising executive to a TV host, well, there were a lot of 'No's.' However, I knew without a shadow of a doubt that I was good TV and that TV needed me, so I kept going and now, twenty years later, it's a bona fide fact."

Val's thoughts: "Let Bevy be your inspiration to believe in yourself regardless of your age or circumstance."

...

Can you share a lesson about work ethic you are passionate about?

Harry Carson: "One of the lessons I try to share with young people is whatever you do, always give your best. As long as you give your best and your all, you can sleep well at night, and so when I played those teams that beat up on us, those were humbling experiences. If you give your all, people see it, recognize it, and appreciate it. To this day, people who see me will say thanks for what you did with the Giants when they were low and weren't all that great."

Val's thoughts: "This puts me at ease when I find myself stressing over perfection. As long as I did my best, that's what counts."

...

Can you dive into your role on the Giants as captain and a defensive player?

Harry Carson: "I helped to resurrect the defense to be a formidable group of guys that wanted to play. People just like your dad, they probably yelled at the TV when the Giants fumbled the ball. My thing was, let me just give my all, and if I give my all, there's nothing more that I can do. It was trying to lead by example: working with guys in helping them to get the best out of themselves and always stay humble. It's humbling when you go out there

> and you initially think you are great and somebody knocks you off your perch."
>
> Val's thoughts: "When you are a pro athlete, you are subject to ridicule. Everyone faces it, but it's how you handle the negative comments, which Harry Carson has clearly done gracefully."

Kindness, connecting, and conviction has helped me in everyday scenarios and it can do the same for you. This next story falls into the category of expect the unexpected, as there was a big annoyance we were able to avoid because I didn't take no for an answer.

During a recent winter holiday vacation with my family, we went to pick up our rental car that we had reserved. The plan was to drive from San Diego to Palm Springs. When we arrived to pick up the vehicle, we were told there was a shortage of vehicles, with no information provided as to when or if one would become available. I quietly slipped away from my mother, brother, and the rest of the crowd, since there were a lot of other people in this situation, and I found the decision maker. I treated him with respect, explained our predicament, and asked for his assistance in the matter. Before I knew it, I was waving my mother and brother over to the vehicle. We got in the car and drove on to Palm Springs thanks to my persistence and asking him for help, instead of criticizing the situation.

VAL'S EVALUATION: "TENACITY TALKS"

An attitude of determination is highly respected and valued. Putting in the work and not giving up even when the journey is a challenging one is exemplary behavior of someone who will succeed. "Don't Be Afraid" and do whatever it takes to make your dreams your reality. As your confidence and network grow, you will elevate to the next level seamlessly. Remember: tenacity talks.

CHAPTER SIX

OVERCOMING SELF-DOUBT

Have you ever found yourself in a predicament where you were doubting yourself? It has likely happened to most of us. In situations where you were self-critical of your performance or receiving constructive criticism from others, take it in stride and turn it into a learning opportunity. What's interesting is that sometimes the judgment stems from our inner voice and we are the ones that are putting unnecessary pressure on ourselves. Don't let this doubt or confusion drown you; instead, take a breath, relax, assess, and revisit the situation when you are thinking more clearly. Try not to overanalyze and avoid questioning your decisions. Move forward, and, instead of beating yourself up, build yourself up.

While reflecting on my personal victories and losses, I started to question myself. I remember getting a C on one of my public speaking presentations when I was in college, and now I'm being asked to speak as the expert and figurehead in my field of communications throughout top universities around the country, including Columbia, the University of Florida, and various New York-based institutions, as well as nonprofit senior communities. While it is important to take feedback from an educator in order to progress, never let the commentary make you feel like you aren't capable. As I am writing this book, I further believe in myself. These opportunities have been so fulfilling and proved to be another outlet where I could share my expertise to affect others positively.

Producing, hosting, and attending events with some of the wealthiest and most selfless philanthropists and accomplished individuals is one of the facets of my work. Many have personally approached me to tell me that my positive energy lights up the room and they want to be around me for that reason. Through aligning and building friendships with my ***"Confidence Community,"*** which I continue to grow, I see my ability to assemble a beautiful, well-rounded group of friends and offer their expertise to my readers as a tangible accomplishment, which helps me push through my self-doubt.

Additional strategies to conquer my uncertainty are remaining curious, creative, and determined. Through my efforts, I was able to produce a live, intimate Oscar viewing event at the iconic Bryant Park Hotel, which garnered press coverage in the *New York Post*'s Page Six column; cohost the ACE Gala at the St. Regis Hotel in support of Empowering the Unhoused; and serve as the spokesperson for the Natural Diamond Council. All of those opportunities were ones I secured through my commitment to reach my goals. Partnering with large stores and brands like JCPenney and the YMCA became my reality, as I took over Joe Jonas' live social channels and shopped with underserved youth to brighten their holidays. Cohosting and producing my podcast, *The AV Effect*, uplifts, entertains, and creates a safe place for vulnerability, featuring chats with lots of my famous friends, including many from my ***"Confidence Community."***

Can you talk to us about self-doubt and being harsh on ourselves?

Dr. Robi Ludwig: "There is a wealth of insightful research about self-doubt. It's been suggested that, at times, we may know too much about ourselves, leading us to be overly critical of who we are and what we're capable of. This is why it may be beneficial to appreciate the kind words others think and say about us and our abilities. The thinking is that others may be able to see some of our assets better than we can at times. Self-doubt can also push us out of our comfort zone, moving us into new situations, which can be a positive for us."

Val's thoughts: "There is so much pleasure that comes from making your friends and those you care about most feel special. Being inclusive is a wonderful way to help circulate a positive uplifting energy that can be felt by the entire room."

...

Have you ever doubted yourself or been doubted by someone else? Please explain the scenario and how you persevered.

Dale Moss: "Many times, but it usually starts after I get into something. I rarely enter into a space unless I feel very certain I will have success, but then comes the learning curve and also the unforeseen or uncontrollable circumstances. Take time for yourself to understand where this doubt, disbelief, or worry is coming from. You need to understand your emotions and feelings. Then, surround yourself with healthy environments that are inspiring and with people that charge your battery."

Val's thoughts: "Understanding why we feel a certain way and where these feelings are stemming from is very important and can help us to respond instead of react."

...

Countess Luann de Lesseps: "All the time, but I never let that stop me. Let's take my own cabaret show *Countess And Friends*, for example. When I started writing it, and working with my first director Ben Rimalower, we had no idea that it would become what it is today. We took a huge chance. We could have crashed and burned, but I rose like a phoenix. At this point, in life, I know what I want, and I'm not afraid to get it."

Val's thoughts: "'Don't Be Afraid', that's what I am talking about!"

...

Vernon Davis: "I think the most obvious answer to those who have followed my career would be my dispute with Coach Mike Singletary in my third year with the San Francisco 49ers. The whole situation was so public, I felt so humiliated at that time. Years later, I realized how that event was good for me and learned something valuable. This significant event forced me not only to become a better player and teammate, but also a better person, which, in turn, made me have the career I did in the National Football League."

Val's thoughts: "For those of you that aren't aware of the scenario, Vernon is referring to a time early in his NFL career where his behavior resulted in being asked to leave the field by his coach. Sometimes, people are quick to react in the moment, especially when the stakes are high; however, it's clear to me that Vernon used this as an opportunity for growth and to create space for himself. In the end, his football career flourished through using this time when he felt self-doubt as a learning opportunity."

...

Isaac Boots: "I am sure many people have doubted me, and I know some people who have told me they do. I just learn to block out the noise and never doubt myself. Your own opinion is worth more than anyone else's because you have to live from your position, not theirs."

Val's thoughts: "Isaac's outlook is one we should all adopt."

...

Jen Selter: "Absolutely. In the world of social media, you have to develop a thick skin. I've learned that rejection is often just redirection. No matter how hard you try, you can't please everyone. What's important is staying true to yourself, learning from the setbacks, and pushing forward. Self-doubt is natural, but perseverance is key."

Val's thoughts: "I'm with Jen: persevere, and don't let anything or anyone stop you."

...

Adam Weitsman: "I doubt myself every day as do others. I persevered every day by showing results."

Val's thoughts: "Results offer tangible proof that you can reflect on when self-doubt arises."

...

Ty Hunter: "Oh, absolutely! There have been moments when self-doubt crept in, and I've faced skepticism from others. When I step out of my comfort zone, I embrace my fears. Now, I feel a rush of excitement when faced with a little fear, as it allows me to learn more about myself and break through boundaries."

Val's thoughts: "Using excitement as fuel for your mission is a great way to rise above self-doubt."

...

Rob Shuter answered—"Oh, I've definitely doubted myself, and I've been doubted by others, too; it's pretty much a rite of passage in any creative field. I was constantly battling that inner voice that said, 'Who do you think you are? Why would anyone care about your stories?'

At the same time, I was also dealing with external doubts from people who didn't outright say, 'You can't do this,' but their skepticism was loud and clear. Things like, 'Oh, so you're still writing that book?', or 'What's your backup plan?'

There was one particular conversation with someone close to me, where they basically said, 'It's really hard to make it as a writer, maybe you should think about something more stable.' They weren't trying to be hurtful, but hearing that from someone I cared about really stung. It made me second-guess everything I was working toward. I started to feel like maybe they were right, that I was chasing something too far out of reach.

But here's how I persevered: I leaned into the doubt, both mine and theirs. I used it as fuel. Instead of letting it make me smaller, I asked myself, 'What if they're right?' And then the follow-up question: 'But what if they're wrong?' I realized that the only way to know for sure was to keep going, to prove to myself—not anyone else—that I could do this.

I created a routine, writing every day, even on the days when I felt like giving up. I reminded myself that everyone who's ever achieved something meaningful has been in this place—doubting themselves or doubted by others. That voice telling me I wasn't good enough didn't disappear, but I learned to keep writing through it. And, eventually, the wins came. Small wins at first—finishing chapters, getting positive feedback from beta readers. Those little moments were enough to keep me going until bigger things started happening.

What I learned from that experience is that doubt doesn't mean you're on the wrong path; in fact, it often shows you're pushing yourself into something new and uncomfortable, which is where growth happens. The key was recognizing that the doubt—mine or anyone else's—didn't define my ability: I did. Persevering meant showing up, even when I wasn't sure if the outcome would be what I hoped for, and in the end, the process itself made me stronger, more determined, and, ultimately, more confident in my voice as a writer."

Val's thoughts: "Being inquisitive and leaning into the what if, in terms of receiving a positive outcome worked for Rob, and it can work for you."

...

Do you ever feel pressure because of the name you built for yourself? And when you are approached and applauded, how do you handle being so well-known for so long?

Harry Carson: "I really don't think about that. If there is something I can do to help someone, and

> if someone approaches me and they need assistance in doing something, I'm a helper and I'm about giving back, because people said the right things to me when I was at these forks in the road and, I ask myself how is it that I wound up parlaying my playing in high school, to earning a scholarship and then going to college and being drafted to play with the New York Giants, and being a captain for ten of my thirteen seasons."
>
> Val's thoughts: "It's so important to provide advice when asked if you can help others, and Harry is exemplary of that."

The expression smoke and mirrors is defined by Merriam-Webster as "something intended to disguise or draw attention away from an often embarrassing or unpleasant issue."[2] In other words, appearances may be deceiving. By citing an uncomfortable and awkward experience my mom and I had when she was visiting me that we can now find comical, you'll see you probably have it more together than you thought and learn never to compare yourself to others.

A close friend and work associate invited my mom and me to dinner at her luxury condo. We were looking forward to having a nice meal, as I was excited for her and my mom to get to know each other. The assumption was that this beautiful, accomplished woman had it all together, when in reality, it was a facade. It's a rare occasion that I feel awkward in a social setting,

---

2 Merriam-Webster.com Dictionary, s.v. "smoke and mirrors," accessed September 3, 2024, https://www.merriam-webster.com/dictionary/smoke%20and%20mirrors.

and I recall how uneasy I felt for both my mother and myself based on how self-absorbed my friend behaved.

When we arrived at her home, she made us feel anything but welcome. We were confused but I was comfortable enough in my relationship with her (or so I thought) to lead my mom into her living room. There was no food prepared, the set dinner table was for staging purposes and not for eating, and my friend was in a robe instead of clothing. When she finally got her act together and got dressed, she had us accompany her downstairs to the local supermarket to buy dinner. I picked up some sushi and my mom got a cooked chicken. We sat at her kitchen counter where she had a protein cookie. Sometimes, people do such a good job of promoting how they want to be perceived to the world, despite it being opposite of how they actually are. After being blindsided, I never looked at her the same.

Then, there are times when celebrities look to me for my opinion; the day I spent with Khloe Kardashian was one of those times. She was in town for New York Fashion Week and a mutual friend asked if I could accompany her in a public relations capacity to one of the fashion shows. We later had a group lunch, where Khloe asked me to pick the restaurant. It makes me feel good when looked upon as an authority in the lifestyle space, and this certainly VALidated me coming from Khloe. It was a wonderful afternoon and a reminder that if someone with the level of Khloe's success appreciates my opinion and where to spend their time, then I should allow self-doubt to dissipate.

Appearing stylish and polished doesn't always have to require you to spend a lot of money. There have been many moments throughout my career where I received compliments on my appearance. Portraying an aura of confidence and the way you carry yourself is the best finishing touch to any ensemble. One memory that sticks with me was when a supermodel complimented my dress and matching eye makeup. The gala was a black-tie affair where I was interviewing on the red carpet. I smiled, said "Thank you," and thought to myself, *Wow, if she only knew I had spent twenty dollars on this dress!*

When I was cast in my first movie role in a film for *Lifetime*, I was beside myself with excitement. This was a totally foreign experience for me, and when I walked on set, I gave myself a positive self-talk. The monologue I would be delivering on Madison Avenue in a scene beside veteran actors was quite lengthy. Preparation, and circling back to the concept of being my own cheerleader, boosted my confidence and resulted in a glowing and seamless delivery. Meeting a new challenge head-on and performing quite well chipped away at my self-doubt.

The men and women opening the doors of some of the most exclusive venues hold the keys to evenings out where you never know who you will meet. Some of these individuals have become iconic based on their power and persona in nightlife and hospitality. Remember to treat everyone equally and respectfully: the person you perceive as having little power or authority may be the most powerful in the room. By being embraced by these tastemakers in control of the velvet rope, I have fostered influential connections and relationships. The access I have been permitted and the results that follow helped to rid my self-doubt. Whether it's being treated like a VIP guest or an accomplishment that helped you believe in yourself further, relish in those moments.

VAL'S EVALUATION: "OVERCOMING SELF-DOUBT"

We all will encounter the feeling of self-doubt at one time or another. Remember that pulling yourself out of your slump if you didn't perform as well as you would have liked is in your control. Learn from your mistakes and recognize that if you aren't selected for a position you applied for, that is not necessarily reflective of your ability. Use the let down as growth, clear your mind and focus. By having shared how myself and my ***"Confidence Community"*** shed and conquer self-doubt, you will realize you are capable of transforming it into confidence.

CHAPTER SEVEN

UTILIZE YOUR RESOURCES

Using a barter system is an effective way for you to utilize your resources. This process creates what I like to refer to as "the boomerang effect." The importance of adding to your list of contacts is key in growing your pool of experts. When in need of a service, take a moment to think about your personal network and how to make use of those in your inner circle. However, be sure you are ready to share what value you can bring to them, as well, and offer to help them in some way so it can be mutually beneficial. Even the most successful people with multiple businesses use this system, including those in my ***"Confidence Community."***

It's been illustrated in this book that making connections leads to prospering personally and professionally. My brother has a work associate whose wife is a professor of journalism and was looking for speakers to share their knowledge and experience with her classroom, and my brother recommended me. Presenting my personal story to these students was invigorating and a confidence builder.

At the time, I was in search of an intern to assist me with my work. The journalism department informed me that the college would offer credit to a student that would intern for me. The enthusiasm and inquisitive disposition that the students displayed was thrilling especially when I received approval that I could select from this pool of candidates. This speaking engagement ended up providing me with the opportunity to mentor and receive support in return. This connection came full circle and benefited the professor, the students, my intern, and myself.

When traveling for work to new places, the priority is to complete the job and perform as sharply as possible, but being able to explore the city is an added plus. This is exactly what happened to me after I opted to chat with a fellow passenger on a connecting flight from LAX to Sacramento. Having less than forty-eight hours in Sacramento, my new friend and her husband picked me up from my hotel and gave me a personal tour of the Northern California winery scene. In return, I was able to reciprocate their kindness by inviting them to a comedy show after receiving an invite from comedian Tommy Davidson who I'd connected with earlier that same day. Being open to making new friendships when you are traveling can completely elevate your experience: my initial friendly gesture of reaching out and making a connection resulted in a fabulous day.

Please give examples of where you collaborated or bartered with someone that could offer you services and was beneficial to both of you.

Adam Weitsman: "Yes, we have been able to trade assistance with financing a real estate project for

> social media and other digital marketing services for my company."
>
> Val's thoughts: "Adam has over 17 million followers, so this trade has proven to yield exceptional results."
>
> ...
>
> Bevy Smith: "My entire business, Dinner with Bevy, is based around collaboration. It started with connecting music artists with fashion brands and has branched out into creating synergies between executives and nonprofits, actors, and art institutions; the entire business is based on a mutually beneficial and organic connection."
>
> Val's thoughts: "You see, tons of successful entrepreneurs have bartered and traded services. It works for them, and it can work for you."

My dear friend, mentor, and member of my ***"Confidence Community"*** Rob Shuter has emphasized to me the importance of being transparent when you ask someone for a favor. Even if requesting help is out of your comfort zone, the end result will prove worthwhile. Be sure to make it clear that it's a mutual transaction, as I mentioned earlier. Have a conversation expressing interest in their needs and note that your assistance and expertise will be available to them in return, even if it takes place in the future.

Specific credentials are needed to break into a career and evolve as an expert in the field. In the next part of this chapter,

I'm going to describe how the barter system has been beneficial to me. Without my reel (a compilation of on-air work highlights), it would make it next to impossible to secure auditions. Everyone's path is different, of course, and my journey began in search of someone who was both a qualified camera operator and an editor to film my reel. The requirements included the ability to record me conducting interviews at red carpet events and edit the footage based on my creative direction. By assisting me, they received access to red carpet events and were able to build their creative portfolio and credentials.

While I didn't have the budget to compensate this talented editor for his hard work, I was able to help him learn how to navigate these types of high caliber events. Sharing my professional relationships and introducing him to the gatekeepers of celebrity event production in New York City was of high value to him. Our arrangement worked so well that we ended up collaborating for several years. Working with others that have different talents than yourself is a game changer and will enable you to get to the next level and then benefit your teammate. Of course, as soon as paid opportunities came up, he was my first phone call. As our work relationship developed, we elevated each other in our respective roles.

Your personal network will grow as you meet more people in your field. The idea is to put yourself out there and not be hesitant. People are attracted to confidence and being addressed with a strong handshake. Speaking with conviction when addressing someone new will spark interest in what you have to say.

Another experience where a mutual transaction worked for me was when I was at a picnic. There were a handful of other celebrations and gatherings in the park, including a little girl's birthday. One of the moms at the party had been my colleague years previously, when I was working as a publicist. After greeting each other, we enjoyed reminiscing about our days at the public relations firm. During our chat, she mentioned she was head of communications for H&M. The popular apparel line is on-brand with the content I present on television, and I wear it all the time, both at work and in my day-to-day routine. She generously offered to connect me with her showroom representative on the spot after I'd mentioned that I'm a fan of the label. When I arrived at the showroom, they had pulled clothes for me in advance and offered me snacks and coffee, truly making it a special experience. As the reciprocal barter, I wore it on television, providing them with visibility and then promoted their brand across my social media platforms. In this case, I was able to instantaneously pay it forward with my posts; however, it is important to take into account that sometimes the barter or "boomerang effect" takes time.

Often, I receive outreach from businesses and brands looking to develop a relationship with me, and this VALidates my worth as an expert. When Mia Wagner Salon in New York City initially asked me to come in and try their haircare services, I was happy to oblige. As most would agree, finding the perfect salon can be challenging, so I was so lucky we found each other. Without question, I, of course, posted my fresh locks and style on social media, crediting the well known salon. When I was approached and offered my own column Spillin' with Val, in *Hamptons Storyboard* magazine, this was when I was able to pay it forward a little further, by featuring the salon in the print edition. Over time, I was able to reciprocate the salon with additional promotional opportunities.

An interesting anecdote is that the salon also caters to celebrity clientele, including Representative Nancy Pelosi. When attending the Global Citizen Festival, I spotted Nancy in the VIP tent and I said the name "Mia Wagner Salon." That's all she needed to hear before waving me over and telling her security to allow me to speak with her.

As a gal about town, I have mastered the art of combining work and pleasure. Oftentimes, when I am out and about, I focus on capitalizing and developing new relationships. Supermodel Tyson Beckford and I had met on several occasions when watching football at sports venues. His friendly and supportive demeanor led me to think of him as a potential host when Rob Shuter and I teamed up to produce Naughty Gossip media industry cocktail parties. The press at that event highlighted Tyson's hosting skills, which broadened their awareness to his other talents. The first event went so well, that when Rob and I got a sponsored deal for the next one, we worked with Tyson again. With Tyson's celebrity and talent, Rob's media persona, and my ability to connect the dots, all parties involved received value in the barter. By utilizing our resources, people wanted to be a part of the guest list, including *Bravo Housewives*, *Vanderpump Rules* cast members, and network TV anchors. We created an event from the ground up, which you are completely capable of doing in your own field.

When you want to kick off your own project, it is essential to be resourceful. That is exactly what I did when I began my podcast, *The AV Effect*. My cohost in the venture, Emmy-winning journalist Alicia Quarles, and I made lists and cross-referenced them in effort to secure notable guests that the audience we were building would resonate with. Through the connections, we developed our ability to break news, which garnered mentions of our podcast in the press, including *The New York Post*.

It is important to keep your eyes open to see who is in front of you and your thinking cap on as an entrepreneur. As my persona as a TV personality and podcaster grew, close friends began organically approaching me to collaborate. My friend, who made a name for himself in the hospitality public relations space, approached us to partner with his clients who own and operate various party venues in New York City. We all put our heads together to produce a Kentucky Derby viewing podcast party. Everyone involved took on a role, and by connecting, communicating, and staying creative, the event was a huge success for all parties involved. Our strong Rolodex of guests, interactive most stylish hat contest, top-tier food and beverages, and making sure each guest felt welcomed and like a VIP were the strategies we used to make this happen. With this, our goals to gain visibility for the venue, add listeners to the podcast, and create brand awareness for our sponsors were all successfully met.

You never know who may be sitting in the seat next to you. One night, I was at a nightclub, and a glass fell and shattered into my leg, resulting in a trip to the emergency room and stitches in my leg. Throughout the week my injury was healing, I was sitting outside in my courtyard and I started to chat with the person sitting next to me. During the course of our conversation, he revealed that he was an emergency room resident. Since I wanted to avoid going back to the emergency room or urgent care, he was kind enough to take them out for me in the comfort of my own apartment. Clearly, this was a connection that simplified my ordeal and a prime example of how I utilized my resources.

VAL'S EVALUATION: "UTILIZE YOUR RESOURCES"

We all have different skill sets. Having people accessible to you that you can barter and trade with, will also allow you to bond and enhance your relationships. By sharing your attributes, you will open doors for yourself and those around you. Be sure to collaborate, don't compete. Everyone wins with the "boomerang effect."

CHAPTER EIGHT

SHARPEN YOUR LISTENING SKILLS

Being a good listener can open up many doors and make those you are engaging with feel respected and valued. For some of us, good listening comes more naturally; for others, myself included, we have to work at it to be more present. Taking a moment and slowing down, in effort to stop your mind from racing ahead, is a contributing factor when it comes to being present and truly listening to the context of the conversation. Improvisation is a fun exercise you can engage in to work on your listening skills, but it's also a great bonding technique among friends. Activities where you can rehearse being present is essential to be able to hone in further on listening.

A powerfully surprising moment that has stuck with me was when I was approached at a charity event by a member of Freestyle Love Supreme, an improvisational hip-hop comedy musical group started by Lin-Manuel Miranda. It took a moment to remember him, but once he shared our first meeting, the picture he painted was crystal clear—our first encounter had been brief, but clearly left an impression on him. He reminded me that, in the early days of his career, he was an intern and he had made a delivery to my apartment. He had some trouble finding my unit, since all of the buildings looked alike, and he remembered how I didn't get frustrated with him by his delay and repeated phone calls. At the event where we were reunited, he relayed to me that my patience and listening to his predicament and being understanding when he was nervous that he was inconveniencing me made him feel respected. Listening to how he volunteered this information, and actually went out of his way to share that when he saw me at this event, made my heart full. Being a good listener will allow those around you to feel worthy and confident, and I love that he achieved his dream to be on Broadway.

As an entertainment correspondent, my assignment includes developing questions based on the program I am reporting for. When you listen and focus on how the interviewee is responding to said questions, they may open a whole new door for you to gather new information and exclusive content. The same goes for conversations where opportunities may arise because you are being a good listener. Below are some examples when being a good listener opened doors for me professionally and enabled charitable initiatives.

When I first moved to New York City, I was received a lot of event invitations and wanted to expand my network socially. This afforded me the opportunity to meet promoters and people in the nightlife scene quite often. One evening, I heard a promoter in search of a location to host a *Saturday Night Live* after-party. I had listened to what someone was in need of, and was able to provide a solution through my network. The perfect venue came to mind, and the owner (who had expressed to me he was looking for celebrity foot traffic) was happy to keep his place open extra late for that kind of comedic star power. *SNL*'s Keenan Thompson and Colin Jost were in attendance, and after the party, my then-roommate and I had an early breakfast with Colin and an actor friend of his. When I recently attended a party Colin was hosting, I gently reminded him of our breakfast. He came back with a cute remark: "Breakfast, that's being generous," since we were out all night having lots of laughs.

Listening provided me with this one-of-a-kind opportunity to book the *SNL* after-party, and I was compensated by the promoter for my work. Seeing Colin after all that time and reflecting on where we are now was very fulfilling.

Can you explain the positive impact becoming a better listener can have?

Adam Weitsman: "Good listening is critical to understanding any and all situations; if you don't listen to who it is you are interacting with, how can you possibly build a good relationship with that person? Listening is critically important, way more so than speaking."

Val's thoughts: "This makes complete sense to me, and it's why I wrote the chapter on it."

...

Dr. Robi Ludwig: "With more insight into a person, we can decide whether they fit or deserve a place in our lives. We can choose to include or exclude people, which is also a form of self-love

> and self-care. Listening is also powerful because it demonstrates to others in our lives that they are heard and valued. Listening is a rare form of attention and respect, which, unfortunately, many people no longer offer to each other. This lack of listening and connecting on a deeper level could also be contributing to the loneliness epidemic so prevalent in our society right now. Knowing that we are capable of listening to others should boost our self-esteem and self-worth; it's also a rare asset to have these days. Active listening will help us be perceived as valuable by others."
>
> Val's thoughts: "Active listening will make the person you are interacting with feel important and can improve relationships overall."

Dr. Robi Ludwig was on the cover of a health magazine, and I attended the celebration in support of her fabulous achievement. Dr. Robi Ludwig is always an amazing party host and surrounds herself with a stellar group of individuals. My ears perked up when I overheard that makeup guru and entrepreneur Laura Gellar was in attendance. As soon as I spotted Laura, an icon in the beauty industry, I approached her and introduced myself. Her products have been highlighted on television segments I was the spokesperson for. We had previously acknowledged each other on Instagram, and now we were meeting in person. She embraced my hello with her warmth, kindness, and down-to-earth spirit right from the start. Our friendship has since flourished and my initial in person contact sparked the relationship. If I wasn't being a good listener and paying attention to my surroundings, I might have missed meeting Laura and not have her as someone I now call a great friend.

During the pandemic, I started my Instagram Live series called "Lifestyle Chats with Val and Friends." One of my interviews that stood out to demonstrate my listening skills was my interview with my friend, original *Real Housewife of New York* Jill Zarin. At the time, she and her daughter Ally were sending meals to hospital staff all around the country to show support for their crucial work combatting COVID.

As my guest, she indicated her difficulty in contacting an administrator at Elmhurst Hospital in Queens, New York which was one of the hardest hit hospitals. I mentioned that I had a friend affiliated with this hospital and I was able to make the connection between them. Jill was listening and I was listening, and that is why the conversation went the direction it did. Days later, care packages were delivered and the hospital hallways experienced moments of joy during the darkest times. This all came from listening, putting the dots together, and making the connection.

By this point in the book, it must seem obvious to you that bringing strangers together and connecting them is part of my nature. While on a bike tour during my first visit to Paris, I was surrounded by other tourists. A bonus for being with fellow travelers was getting to know people from all different cultures, as the group was comprised of visitors from all over the world. A great icebreaker was to volunteer to take a photo for your fellow participants. We all wanted to create memories and a simple, kind gesture would likely have them return the small favor when you would like to capture a magical moment with the ones you love most.

Having opted to chat with a woman on the tour, we both quickly realized that we worked in television and had a handful of mutual connections. She was about to embark on her new role as an executive on *The Jennifer Hudson Show* when she returned home from Paris. We have remained in contact via email, and what I love is that being a good listener steered the conversation toward uncovering what we have in common and creating an instant bond. You never know what the future holds and when our paths will circle back in a potential work and personal setting. When I had the privilege of interviewing Jennifer Hudson for an *E! News exclusive* it was an excellent ice breaker and Jennifer loved hearing the story.

Marketing in support of your own brand is a great way to further your career, build confidence, and make new connections. A longtime friend of mine and her husband started an athleisure clothing brand, and they would send me samples to promote on my platform. After featuring a few different designs, it dawned on me we could work together on a #youvebeenVALidated customized version of leggings. If you don't ask, you don't get, and this is a phrase you should remember and one that produced my own branded merchandise.

In business, you can discover new opportunities through word-of-mouth, so when I began to hear chitchat about a new video development distribution platform, I began doing my research by asking around and being a good listener and not sitting on the sidelines. When I was introduced to a member of the publication looking to launch broadcast content at a book launch party, I inquired about their new venture into broadcasting. After submitting my credentials to the editor, he put me in touch with the head of video, who I then met with. That meeting went well, so he connected me with one of his colleagues heading up the long form series division. Then, I was linked to his head producer, and six months later, as a result of my good listening and persistence, I was filming and producing a pilot with his team for the platform.

VAL'S EVALUATION: "SHARPEN YOUR LISTENING SKILLS"

We are taught early on in school to be good listeners and to pay attention. These are lessons you should take with you throughout life. Slowing down and being present is an excellent way to improve your listening skills, and will enhance your ability to communicate confidently and be heard in return. You will be able to respond to the conversation with clear context and this will enhance the communication and lead to new opportunities.

CHAPTER NINE

THE HARD DAYS

Everyone has hard days, and braving them and pushing through will become a little bit easier by realizing you are not alone. We all experience difficult episodes, and they can range from being as severe as mourning the loss of a loved one, to financial worries, or even just not feeling well. Sometimes, I don't know why I wake up worried or in a bad mood. Sure, it probably has to do with underlying stress and anxiety I have been prone to, but sometimes you don't need a reason to have a hard day. When feeling down and like nothing is going your way, try to let those negative feelings go and refocus your frustration into the positives that can happen at any moment. Releasing what is no longer serving you can be very challenging for many of us; however, putting in the effort to do so will get you on the right track. Feelings and emotions are fleeting; remember this when going through hard times and try to hold onto the good feelings as long as you can.

Can you weigh in on moving through the hard days?

Dr. Robi Ludwig: "It is important to recognize that feeling down is not a sign of failure in life, but rather a sign of our humanity. Emotions provide valuable information. While we may prefer certain emotions over others, it's important to consider what our feelings are trying to communicate about ourselves and our lives. Our emotions can guide us and help us navigate during challenging times."

Val's thoughts: "Feeling strong physically and mentally is extremely helpful during difficult situations that are out of your control. Stop engaging in behaviors that make you compare or feel like you are missing out. Practice uplifting thoughts and actions that work for you. Sometimes a change of environment, calling a friend, a good distraction, or reading a book can be helpful in redirecting negative thoughts. Making a list of what you are grateful for will allow you to overcome these negative thoughts and take your power back. In an effort to redirect my thoughts, I sat down and made a list of all of my recent accomplishments, which was very helpful for me."

...

Can you talk about hard times that you have overcome?

Adam Weitsman: "Challenges are a part of everyday life; it is important to not only recognize them, but proactively work through them, both personally and professionally. I often times will reflect on the situation, evaluate what went wrong, and determine how I can pave the way for a better outcome in the next situation.

Val's thoughts: "Reflection can be a powerful tool."

...

Harry Carson: "The number one challenge that I had coming to play with the New York Giants is that I never played the position they asked me to play, which is very unusual. I had to change my course and play a position that I never really thought I would be playing, and I would have to attribute the switch to my linebacker coach, who thought that I could play a position that he needed to get the defense going, as a middle linebacker. The challenge that I had was to make the transition from being a defensive lineman. When you get to the NFL and you change positions, you have to know what everybody has to do because, in essence, you become the quarterback and eventually the captain of the defense. I sort of look at everything that is in front of me and I try to look and see if I can defeat those challenges and for the most part, why not, you know, it's just like playing ball. I had the opportunity to play, I could have said, 'No, I can't do this,' but I sort of saw it as a challenge and I tried to give it all I've got to show myself that it can be done and there is not one specific way to get a job done, and there are multiple ways that you can get there."

Val's thoughts: "Harry was taken by surprise and had to learn a whole new set of skills at the elite level. He met this challenge with a can-do attitude and proved that with his mindset, talent, and fierceness as a competitor, he would preVAiL."

...

Jen Selter: "I've learned that during hard times, it's crucial to allow yourself to sit with your emotions and truly feel them. So often, we try to push away the discomfort or pretend we're okay, but acknowledging those feelings is what leads to growth. Every struggle I've faced—whether personal or professional—has made me stronger and more resilient. I remind myself that everything is temporary, and even the toughest challenges eventually pass. There have definitely been moments when I've felt down or doubted myself, but I've come to realize that these moments are often the ones that shape you the most. When I find myself in a tough spot, I focus on small steps to rebuild my energy. Whether it's through a workout, journaling, or simply taking a break to breathe, I reconnect with what brings me peace. Each setback has allowed me to see new opportunities that I might have missed otherwise. Sometimes, what feels like an obstacle is actually a chance to redirect and grow in ways you never imagined. What keeps me going is knowing that challenges don't define you—they refine you. And when you come out the other side, you're not the same person you were before; you're stronger, wiser, and more ready for what's ahead."

Val's thoughts: "Jen is absolutely right and, as I mentioned in the beginning of the book, sitting with our emotions and feeling them can be scary and sometimes it seems easier to push them away, however this is only a temporary fix."

...

Paula Froelich: "Life is not linear. I learned that the hard way: my life has been up and down and up and down, and it's helped me because every time I'm down, I remember it will go back up again, and it's going to be okay."

Val's thoughts: "Feelings are impermanent and don't last forever, and as we fall on challenges and hard times, we have to remember that they will pass."

Making the best out of an unpleasant situation may be challenging, but it is better than the alternative. When riding the train from Santa Barbara to LA, after a beautiful day of events with my family, there was a lot of activity taking place out of my control: fellow passengers were being loud and obnoxious, and they pulled the emergency break, which delayed our trip. It was difficult to relax with all of this commotion going on; however, my mom, who was sitting next to me, suggested I distract myself and reset my emotions of anger and annoyance by reading, and it worked.

Turning to humor and creativity are also great ways to lift your spirits when you have racing thoughts about your future and what comes next. Waiting for someone to make a decision that will affect your business can be very trying on your nerves. While you're waiting, use your time productively to create more potential opportunities for yourself. Speaking to friends who have been candid about losing their jobs (and how not stewing in their own sorrows for too long helped them move forward) is the right attitude to have. A great exercise for getting your mindset right is creating a vision board for yourself. Relishing in this visual reminder is an excellent way to spend your time.

Fighting for payment is something many businesses face, and, as an entrepreneur, I have encountered this. It's unfortunate that people sometimes don't pay their bills on time for services provided; however, it is important that you don't let your feelings of stress overcome you when this happens. Of course, do everything you can to advocate for your compensation, and if you still don't receive payment, be sure not to work with them again. Then, move on to the next item on your checklist and don't let it consume you.

When you work on a project for a long time, one you are optimistic about for good reason, receiving positive feedback that ends up being full of false promises, a feeling of disappointment is inevitable. I found myself in this predicament, being led on after putting in an immense amount of time and effort into creating a project with so much potential. The day I found out we weren't moving forward was a very hard day, based on my passion for the creation and the interest that was expressed from the other end. However, how I healed from this was by choosing to take away what I learned throughout the process, as I am now equipped with additional skills.

Being able to wing it when your plans don't go smoothly is imperative. Remain calm and find a solution regardless of the obstacles in your way. Go with the flow, step out of the box, and revise your plan however makes the most sense in the moment. Don't spoil the experience for yourself and the others around you; be flexible and innovative. Emanating positive energy can go a long way and be a solution in itself, and use the glitches as a learning experience to keep going.

The obvious answer may have been in front of you and you didn't see it; however, don't dwell on what you missed, keep going and learn from the experience. By choosing to be a proponent of growth and seeking new opportunities, I've reaped multiple benefits. Regardless of where you live, your expenses and the cost of living can be very challenging to navigate. I explored new work avenues when finances were tight. While looking through online databases that provide listings of open castings, Casting Networks jumped off the page, and I began submitting myself for background work opportunities for employment. Here is the timeline of how quickly things can move: I sent my details in on a Tuesday, received a text from the casting director on Wednesday checking my availability, and was cast for the series *And Just Like That...* on Thursday. Be open to areas of work in your field you didn't consider previously. For me, doing acting background work was a new experience, a way to make extra money, and connect with new people. In retrospect, I could have beaten myself up for not exploring this avenue sooner, but I quickly reset my thinking to realize that would be self-sabotage, and instead transformed my hard day into a fantastic day.

Were you ever so close to a project being greenlit you could taste it, and then, without any explanation, it didn't come to fruition? Please explain how you turned your lemons into lemonade in this scenario.

Isaac Boots: "I do believe that you have to have an attitude of what is meant to be will be. If it is the right project for you, it will go. If it doesn't, then it probably was not for you anyways. That type of acceptance in this very crazy and tough business will serve you better than any project. Being a professional dancer, you will hear 'no' so many more times than you will hear 'yes,' so accepting rejection is essential to really becoming successful."

Val's thoughts: "In business dealings, not everything is in our control. Getting comfortable accepting rejection, not letting it get us down, and recognizing it isn't a reflection of our capabilities is key."

VAL'S EVALUATION: "THE HARD DAYS"

We are all going to experience letdowns in life. It is helpful to remember that emotions are fleeting, especially during the low moments. Mental health, stress, and anxiety are factors that can play significant roles during hard days. It is important to try to handle these challenges with grace and dignity, which is healthier for us in the end. Don't be afraid to ask others for help; that is a strength, not a weakness.

CHAPTER TEN

WHAT CONSTITUTES SUCCESS?

The meaning of success is different for everyone. Merriam Webster defines success as "favorable or desired outcome; *also*: the attainment of wealth, favor, or eminence."[3] Social media often projects images of perfection, and can make us feel like meeting our goal is not within reach. Personal feelings of success can run the gamut of, "Did I win the high school track meet?" all the way to "Am I number one on the bestseller list?" After conferring with my ***"Confidence Community,"*** this question garnered very personal responses, all of which are correct, since this is subjective and based on their own life's journey. For me, some of my self-thoughts that come up regarding success are, "Am I doing enough? Am I doing this right?"

As you have seen in this book, the quality of your network can add power to what you can achieve. If you are wondering if you should take the leap toward your passion, I say go for it!

3 Merriam-Webster.com Dictionary, s.v. "success," accessed September 30, 2024, https://www.merriam-webster.com/dictionary/success.

Set yourself up to win to the best of your ability, and here are some suggestions how you can do that through connections and confidence:

1. The more awareness of your surroundings you have, the more opportunities you will notice.
2. The expression "word of mouth" carries weight. There have been many times that my professional and personal network looped me into new opportunities.
3. Teaching yourself to be brave is also a form of success, by taking the leap to move forward toward achieving your goals.
4. Remember that there is no victory that is too small to celebrate. Each little step will help you build your inner growth and your tree of success.

When I come across entry-level professionals, I notice that they often put the word "just" in front of their title, as in, "I'm just an intern," or "I'm just an assistant." For those that are engaging in this behavior, reframe your thought process. You are an integral part of the team. You are the foundation of the structure and provide value. Remind yourself of this whenever you need to hear it. That is a form of success.

When you find yourself getting frustrated or stuck, remember that it only takes one "yes!" Take it from Lady Gaga as she said, "There could be one hundred people in one room and ninety-nine don't believe in you, and all it takes is one person to believe in you and that could change everything." Stop worrying what others think of you, unless it's that one, of course! Self-improvement is constant and the work never stops, so make sure to have a positive association with this.

Imagine being fairly new to the New York City social scene and then reading about yourself in the *New York Daily News*. This happened to me and will always remain a special moment in my life. As a freelance reporter working on the red carpet at the Songwriters Hall of Fame for *Us Weekly*, Grammy winner John Mayer interrupted an interview he was in the middle of to pay me a compliment. This was overheard by another reporter and ended up in print. It made me feel good to be recognized by this major celebrity and raised my confidence level. A few months later while out and about, I saw him at an event and was able to thank him for his comment and its effect on me.

What does success mean to you?

Dr. Robi Ludwig: "The psychological definition of success can vary greatly. Success is a term that holds different meanings for different individuals. For some, success may entail achieving a certain level of financial stability or professional accomplishment. For others, success may involve having a fulfilling personal life or making a positive impact on the world. The definition of success is highly individualistic, as it should be. Personally, I am a firm believer that happiness is equivalent to true success, and when we stop comparing ourselves to other people, it is helpful inaction that will guide you to happiness. Life is about balance."

Val's thoughts: "Think about what makes you truly happy and spend more time on those activities;

also, think about the people who bring you joy and spend more time with them."

...

Adam Weitsman: "Success used to be just financial, but now happiness is everything. You can have all of the financial reward, but if you have no one to share it with and aren't happy, then it's empty."

Val's thoughts: "Through building your own ***"Confidence Community,"*** you'll always have someone special to share your rewards with."

...

Jen Selter: "Success, to me, is about achieving personal fulfillment and balance in all areas of life. It's not just about reaching big milestones or hitting career goals; it's about living in alignment with my values, being happy with the journey, and continuously growing as a person. It's also about making a positive impact—whether that's inspiring others, building meaningful relationships, or contributing to something bigger than myself. Success means feeling proud of what I've accomplished, but even more, feeling content and at peace with where I am, knowing I've stayed true to myself along the way. It's more about progress, not perfection, and enjoying the process while making meaningful connections.

Val's thoughts: "Living authentically allows me to feel successful as well."

...

Vernon Davis: "To me, success is being able to dip my hands in as many avenues as possible. I truly love learning about new industries and creating within those industries."

Val's thoughts: "Vernon does this so exceptionally well by always being open to learning."

...

Rob Shuter: "Success, for me, has shifted over time. When I was younger, I used to think of success as something very external—achieving big career milestones, gaining recognition, or hitting financial goals. But over the years, I've come to see it differently.

Now, success feels more like living a life that feels meaningful and authentic, where the things I do align with who I am at my core. Success means having the freedom to pursue creative projects that excite me and make me feel fulfilled, rather than just doing things for external validation. It's about making a positive impact on others—whether that's through my work, personal relationships, or even small, everyday interactions. If I can help someone feel seen, heard, or understood, that feels like success to me.

On a personal level, success also means having balance. It's being able to spend time with the people I care about, finding joy in the little things, and taking care of my mental and physical health. It's about setting boundaries that allow me to enjoy the present moment instead of always chasing the next big thing.

Ultimately, success is about feeling content with where I am, while still having the curiosity and drive to keep growing. It's less about reaching a specific destination and more about the journey—feeling proud of the effort, the growth, and the connections I've made along the way."

Val's thoughts: "Balance is the magic word and so important to incorporate throughout life."

Never second guess your worth based on your financial status. It isn't healthy emotionally to compare your level of monetary success with others. Accept where you are and strive to do better, if that's what you desire. Be proud of your personal and professional accomplishments, and always hold your head high. If you are in pursuit of personal and professional happiness, don't think of just wealth in dollar signs. Think of kindness and your core values as well.

VAL'S EVALUATION: "WHAT CONSTITUTES SUCCESS?"

Success can be interpreted in many different ways. Oftentimes, it is thought of or perceived as the amount of money someone has or their ranking in their career and social status. Think about what success means to you and that will help you to attain your goals and live a balanced happy life.

CHAPTER ELEVEN

REAPING YOUR REWARDS

Rewarding yourself for your achievements is a great way to stay motivated. Take time to reflect and appreciate your efforts toward getting closer to your goals. Celebrate small and big wins and welcome those you care about most to share in them with you.

For me personally, creating special moments with my family is an extraordinary way to spend time. It truly is what's most important to me. My brother surprised me with a trip to Spain with him and my mother for my birthday. Upon arrival after an overnight flight, while waiting for our room to be ready, my mom decided to relax in the One hotel's lobby, while my brother powered up his computer to do some work. I, on the other hand, decided to explore the amenities that were available, and found myself at the Zen Lounge and Spa.

This was an example of creating the best scenario for myself by being curious. There, I hit the steam room and sauna and enjoyed tapioca pudding in the meditation lounge. I was provided with a plush robe and slippers and was comfy and pampered. When I came back to the lobby after receiving a text from my brother, my mom was shocked to see me in this relaxed state and started laughing out of confusion since I looked super refreshed. She said, "You sure know how to get taken care of," and we laughed.

Another experience that stood out from that trip was visiting the home that my brother lived in when he was studying abroad. Much to his surprise, the family he stayed with still occupied the same residence. He was able to introduce my mother and myself to someone that was very important in his life when he was in school and they reconnected. This was a feel-good reward for taking us on this trip that he was able to share part of his history with us. It just goes to show that even when people are different and don't have immediate things in common, it doesn't mean you can't create a powerful relationship that affects all parties positively, and that's exactly what that interaction did for all of us that day: dig up pleasant memories to experience them once again. Maybe we will have to take the leap and knock again in twenty years.

Something as small as a magnet can be a conduit to remind yourself of a positive memory in your life. Every time I travel to a new place, I purchase a souvenir to remind myself of the happy moments I have had. Whether it is a small trinket or a splurge that I was able to reward myself with, creating a positive association with the object helps bring memories forth to the surface that evoke endorphins.

Invest in yourself by taking up a new hobby, engaging in a few moments of meditation or grabbing your favorite latte: there is no reward too small. Your efforts matter, and by recognizing your worth with a symbolic action you take for yourself, the positive association will encourage you to keep moving forward.

When you make an initial connection with someone, even if you don't see them on a regular basis, it can be beneficial to check in with them and keep the relationship alive. A few years back, I was a guest at a Mad Hatter themed tea party, and I met the representative of the tequila brand that was sponsoring. After that, we kept seeing each other at various work and social events, as we ran in the same circles, and I always made it my business to say hello. My friendliness was appreciated by her, since she reached out to me, extending an invitation to accompany her front row and with an all access pass to see Aerosmith in concert. It just so happened that that was one of their final performances. The thrill of being front row and crowned an Aerosmith Angel with an all access pass, which included being on stage and escorted to different parts of the performance sections so we could see everything up close and personal, had endorphins pumping throughout me and everyone I was there with. That kind of talent is so unique and iconic. Saying hello to the tequila representative that day provided me with a once-in-a-lifetime experience.

Can you tell me why it is important to reap your rewards and how you do so?

Adam Weitsman: "The nectars of success are just as important as the spoils of failure, and it is important to feel them both equally. Spending time with loved ones is how I most enjoy celebrating an accomplishment, as those are the ones who are my rock and support me daily."

Val's thoughts: "It seems that my ***"Confidence Community"*** and I share many similar values, as we highly regard spending time with the people most important to us."

...

Isaac Boots: "For me, experiences are how I like to celebrate success. I want to go to Lake Como and stay at Villa d'Este with my husband and my dogs, or take all my best friends out to dinner. The thrill of buying something wears off quickly, but making a special moment with your loved ones and capturing the moment inspires me to keep going. There is no reward if you have no one to share it with, and I am very fortunate to have an amazing group of chosen family."

Val's thoughts: "As I mentioned above, for me, just like Isaac and Adam, making memories with friends and family through shared experiences is when I feel most rewarded."

Debate was one of my favorite subjects in high school as I was growing up in Florida. Working on my presentation skills enhanced my ability to communicate. During parents' night, my mom was sitting in my classroom chair and thought there was a familiar aura about my teacher from her past. At the end of the open house, my mother approached my teacher, who immediately recognized my mother as her student teacher years prior in New York. If my mom hadn't been inquisitive and said hello, the two of them wouldn't have reconnected. My mother's earlier relationship enhanced my high school debate experience and made the class that much more meaningful.

Often, I refer to myself as a "girl on the glow," running into various notable names on multiple occasions. *American Idol* winner Jordin Sparks is represented by my previous work supervisor and friend. While vacationing in Los Angeles with my family, and strolling through the hotel lobby, Jordin was posing for a photo shoot. We chatted about our common connection and love for this person, took a photo, and then went on with our day. A year later, I was at Bergdorf Goodman in New York City for a private event, and there was Jordin and my friend, who remains her publicist. We all had the best time together that evening. Her publicist is aware that I have work relationships with local TV stations and I was able to assist coordinating a future booking for Jordin in support of a performance of hers. Being helpful to someone who was influential to me early on in my career is very rewarding. I was able to help Jordin, her publicist, and the television studio. We all reaped rewards from our connections.

Famed musician Wyclef Jean is a sensational performer. Over the past few years, I have become friendly with a member of his management team and attended his concerts. We all hang out and chat before he goes on stage. One of his songs is a collaboration with Shakira, and I made him aware that my curly hair received some look-alike Shakira comments. When the song came on, he motioned me to the stage. I got to dance on stage with Wyclef and hyped concertgoers up, which was a once-in-a-lifetime experience that was mentioned in *The New York Post*. Fellow audience members caught it on camera, and it is a memory I will forever remember.

There were two evenings I spent with musical icons that warranted waking up my parents in the middle of the night. The night that Britney Spears embraced me is one that will stay ingrained in my memory forever.

I was in the VIP section at this hot celebrity nightclub, Tenjune, and when she walked in most people's jaws hit the floor. My friend, the same club manager who gave me the lead on my apartment, brought Britney into our section. There is no other way to explain it other than the next thing I know, she and I are jumping up and down, dancing and holding hands on a couch. Another evening where my dance moves and hair flips were on full display was at Solange Knowles' private album release party at the Boom Boom Room in New York City. There was a circle of solid dance moves that I was key to igniting, and Beyoncé was a part of it. She was waving her hands in the air, nodding with approval directly at me, while dancing and smiling with me in our circle. This was my moment of VALidation!

Having scored a meeting with a celebrity publicist when I first arrived to New York City continues to resonate with me. I was given an opportunity to express my interest in talent representation and she in turn took time out of her day providing me with guidance as to how to advance toward my goals. Paying it forward is very important to me and when approached by a reporter from Miami looking for direction and advice on how to break into the New York television market I was happy to oblige. This reporter reaches out whenever she visits New York City, and to my pleasant surprise, she extended an invitation to join her at a Broadway play that her parents were producers on. As if that wasn't enough, our seats were front row. This was an exceptional experience and a reward I happily embraced. When I met with her all I wanted was to offer advice that might inspire a young new talent; I didn't expect the amazing friendship that would follow.

VAL'S EVALUATION: "REAPING YOUR REWARDS"

We all deserve to reward and treat ourselves for our hard work, whether it's a day at the spa, a chocolate chip cookie, designer shoes, or a vacation. Remember in elementary school when your teacher gave you stickers or stars to motivate you, and it worked? Promise yourself a special treat as you make personal and professional strides. Reap your rewards and be good to yourself by celebrating your VALU.

POSTFACE

VALIDATED VALU EXERCISES AND GLOSSARY

By modifying your behavior in social settings, you will achieve the outcome you desire when it comes to being a better connector. This can be accomplished by practicing simple exercises I developed based on the chapters of the book. Start by creating a journal dedicated to cultivating new connections, building on existing relationships, and enhancing your confidence.

The following exercises will help you discover your VALU, providing you inspiration and VALidation.

1. Begin by making a list of the new people you engage in conversation with each week. Increase the number as time goes on, and get more detailed on the notes and descriptions you write down based on the interaction for reference. Use this as encouragement to keep moving forward in your efforts to expand your network, develop meaningful relationships, and to be your own best friend.
2. Write yourself a message highlighting your superpower and review it whenever you need a boost of confidence.

3. Take a moment and think about a long term goal you have. Jot it down along with tenacious behavior, effort, and steps you've been taking to get closer to your achievement.
4. When self-doubt arises, challenge the thought. For example, by asking yourself, "Will I have enough time to familiarize myself with the material?" You can ensure you are always prepared, regardless of time constraints, and you'll perform exceptionally!
5. Reach out to three friends or associates with different skill sets than you. Write their names down, along with their expertise. Think about what you can offer them to make the boomerang and barter system come full circle.
6. Engage in a conversation, and listen intently. Assess what the takeaways were and how clear the message was communicated to you. Taking quiet time for yourself will help you clear your mind, improve your patience, and result in you being a better listener.
7. Keep track of situations you find challenging during the hard days. Document what you learned from them and focus on that as the takeaway.
8. Success is subjective, since it has different meanings to all of us. Write down what it means to you. Ask yourself if it has taken on any additional new meanings.
9. Reap your rewards! Go out into the world and take what you've learned by reading this book. Remember to be your own best friend and share your awesomeness with the world.

Design your own personal phrases or superpower messages that are unique to you. Here are a few of my VAL-isms, otherwise known as terms sparking my creativity and confidence, which you have also seen in the material.

1. VALU: You are important and held in high regard.
2. VALium: You are enough! Use this phrase as a reminder to engage in activities that lead you to a calm and confident state
3. VALiant: Use this phrase as encouragement to embrace your challenges
4. PreVAiL: Use this phrase as a reminder that you can accomplish anything. Remember you always have your tenacity and affirmations to lean on
5. eVALuations: meaning—Think of this phrase as a summary or evaluation

WHAT WRITING THIS BOOK MEANS TO ME

My ability to bring new people together and observing how my actions in doing so affect those around me positively, was a strong motivating factor in writing this book, sensing that I could share a message of VALU with others. The evolution of this project began early on in my career, when I would do a self-eVALuation, recognizing my ability to connect people and boost their confidence to help them believe in themselves. My superpower as a communicator has afforded me the ability to enter a room of new people and, by the end of the evening, exit with a handful of new contacts, friends, and other people I've connected amongst themselves. This is a talent and gift I embrace and is so much more powerful by sharing it with the world. While I was building my lifestyle brand #youvebeen-VALidated, observing how I lead my life in social situations, friends would point out my style of communicating and how I would conduct myself would empower them. By embracing and honing in on my unique personal strengths, I found a need for this material.

Making the commitment to writing this book has given me the opportunity to experience personal growth, and I'm proud of how disciplined I've become. This process has evoked all types of emotions for me. Despite feeling nervous, anxious, and even experiencing self-doubt at times, I didn't let that stop me. My tenacious behavior kicked in and kept me moving forward. Revealing more about my life and being vulnerable has been cathartic in a lot of ways. By sharing my story and connecting with you through my words in this book, I hope to leave you inspired. There were life events taking place where I experienced emotional ups and downs that would pull me away from my focus on writing the book, yet I did not waver. The importance of completing this project outweighed all of the outside noise and uncontrolled variables, leaning on my strength and commitment.

By writing my truth and sharing my passion for how I organically navigate life, the messages and chapters throughout this book ring powerfully true for me. My desire is that through creating and always being open to expanding your ***"Confidence Community,"*** you'll learn and build on your confidence and connections. The book may be ending, however, this is just your beginning. #youvebeenVALidated #passiton

ACKNOWLEDGMENTS

Firstly, I want to thank my parents and my brother for their endless love, selflessness, and encouragement. Their support has provided me with the inspiration and can-do attitude to write this book. I love you always and forever! #youvebeenVALidated

Secondly, to my ***"Confidence Community,"*** thank you for playing such a significant role in my life. Taking the time out of your busy lives to answer my questions and be part of this book means so much to me!

Finally, to my friends and work colleagues, thank you for always being by my side and for boosting my belief in myself.

ABOUT THE AUTHOR

Photo by Mark Doyle

Valerie Greenberg is an in-demand national lifestyle expert, pop culture media personality, and television host. As a graduate of the University of Florida's College of Journalism and Communications, she is often called upon as a motivational speaker and expert panelist at universities and symposiums. Her brand, #YouveBeenVALidated, empowers you to channel the most confident version of yourself. Valerie's versatility spans from writing her own magazine column to acting on network and streaming programs, including *And Just Like That* and co-starring on the fall finale of *The Equalizer*. Her television credits include *Good Morning America*, *Extra!*, *Inside Edition*, and *E! News* as well as local news programs. She serves as a brand spokesperson for a variety of beauty and lifestyle brands. Follow Valerie on instagram.com/valgreenberg and visit her website https://youvebeenvalidated.com/.